ANCIENT EGYPTIAN DANCES

IRENA LEXOVÁ

With drawings made from reproductions
of ancient Egyptian originals by
Milada Lexová

Introduction to the Dover Edition by
Diane Bergman
Wilbour Librarian, Wilbour Library of Egyptology
Libraries and Archives, Brooklyn Museum of Art

English translation by
K. Haltmar

DOVER PUBLICATIONS, INC.
Mineola, New York

Copyright

Copyright © 2000 by Dover Publications, Inc.
All rights reserved under Pan American and International Copyright Conventions.

Bibliographical Note

This Dover edition, first published in 2000, is an unabridged republication of the work originally published by the Oriental Institute, Prague, Czechoslovakia, 1935. Fold-outs among the dance drawings have been slightly reduced and reprinted as turn pages. To identify drawings on pages 85–161, the abbreviation "Fig." replaces the original "Obr." throughout.
Diane Bergman's introduction was written specially for the Dover edition.

Library of Congress Cataloging-in-Publication Data

Lexová, Irena.
   [O staroegyptském tanci. English]
   Ancient Egyptian dances / Irena Lexová ; with drawings made from repro-
ductions of ancient Egyptian originals by Milada Lexová ; introduction to the
Dover edition by Diane Bergman ; English translation by K. Haltmar.—
Dover ed.
     p. cm.
   Originally published: Praha, Czechoslovakia : Oriental Institute, 1935.
   Includes bibliographical references.
   ISBN 0-486-40906-6 (pbk.)
   1. Dance—Egypt. 2. Egypt—Social life and customs—To 332 B.C.
3. Dance—Religious aspects. I. Title.

GV1613 .L413 2000
793.3'1932—dc21

                        99-051617

Manufactured in the United States of America
Dover Publications, Inc., 31 East 2nd Street, Mineola, N.Y. 11501

CONTENTS:

INTRODUCTION TO THE DOVER EDITION

Ancient Egypt has been a source of fascination to the modern world since its rediscovery two hundred years ago by Napoleon Bonaparte and his savants. Everything about the pharaonic Egyptians has inspired close study. It started with the visible and obvious like temples and pyramids. Champollion expanded the range of study and in fact gave birth to the scientific field of Egyptology with his decipherment of the hieroglyphic writing of the Egyptians using the Rosetta Stone as the key. Eventually, every minute aspect of ancient Egyptian life became the subject of close scrutiny. Religious worship, burying the dead, slaughtering beef, brewing beer and all other human activities were examined.

The study of dance was no exception to this. The early-published sources on dance are listed by Lexová herself in her introduction. All of these are rather broad in their scope, containing either short sections on dance or scattered references throughout those books. Lexová's book is the first monograph devoted entirely to dance in ancient Egypt. It consists of a corpus of seventy-eight illustrations organized chronologically from the Predynastic Period through the New Kingdom with a few images from the Saite Period, the twenty-sixth Dynasty. The author also includes two images of Etruscan dancers at the end of the book for the purpose of comparison.

Lexová accesses the pictorial material through classification. She catalogs the images into ten types ranging from pure movement to religious and funerary dances. The discussion concludes with the musicians and musical instruments that accompany the dancers.

No book exists in a vacuum and every book is indeed enhanced by its relationship to other books of the same or related topic. Here are collected the most useful publications on dance in ancient Egypt that appeared after the work of Lexová:

Brunner-Traut, Emma. Tanz. IN: Lexikon der Ägyptologie 6. Wiesbaden: Harrassowitz, 1985.

Brunner-Traut, Emma. Der Tanz im alten Ägypten nach bildlichen und inschriftlichen Zeugnissen, dritte, erweitere Auflage (Ägyptologische Forschungen 6) Glückstadt: Verlag J.J. Augustin, 1992. Revision of the two earlier editions of 1937 and 1958.

Decker, Wolfgang, and Herb, Michael. Bildatlas zum Sport im alten Ägypten: Corpus der bildlichen Quellen zu Leibesübungen, Spiel, Jagd,

Tanz und verwandten Themen (Handbuch der Orientalistic I: Der Nahe und Mittlere Osten) Leiden: Brill, 1994.

Vandier, J. La Danse. IN: Manuel d'Archéologie égyptienne 4. Paris: Picard, 1964, p. 391–486.

Wild, Henri. Les danses sacrées de l'Égypte ancienne. IN: Les danses sacrées (Sources orientales 6) Paris: Éditions du Seuil, 1963.

The monograph by Brunner-Traut is the most detailed and complete of this bibliography. The material was refined over many years with unquestioned scholarship. In Brunner-Traut's book are many quotations of the Egyptian literature that accompanied the ancient illustrations, and, in addition to drawings, many photographs of monuments depicting dancers. Lexová's work was written virtually simultaneously, but its form is different and serves as a useful complement to Brunner-Traut.

The fact that the Lexová book is translated into English greatly increases the accessibility to its information. This is the only major work on ancient Egyptian dance in English. Its seventy-eight illustrations are rendered in line drawing making it very clear to see the positions, especially for the recreation of the dance steps.

Much research has been done in the field of ancient Egyptian dance, as in all aspects of Egyptological study, since 1935. Some of Lexová's interpretations have yielded to new insights and understanding, but her drawings remain unsurpassed. There is much overlap of illustrated scenes among Lexová, Brunner-Traut and Decker. If desired, they can be used in conjunction to get a total impression of the steps and positions with the aid of the photographs of the original representations.

In my capacity of Wilbour Librarian, I have had many occasions to introduce students of dance and choreographers to this book. The Wilbour Library is one of the few libraries in the New York metropolitan area that holds a copy. Only seventeen libraries in the United States list it among their holdings in the Research Libraries Information Network (RLIN).

The reaction to seeing this book, especially on the part of choreographers, has been to want to photocopy many of the images. I shall now be able to refer them to this reprint which I heartily welcome.

Diane Bergman
Wilbour Librarian
Wilbour Library of Egyptology
Libraries and Archives
Brooklyn Museum of Art
New York

PREFACE.

Some years ago I saw some modern dancing girls perform Egyptian dances. The common characteristics of all these dances were the insipid, jerky movements, unaesthetic postures, and abrupt turns of limbs. Although some of the girls asserted that it was the ancient Egyptian pictures of Egyptian dancers which they copied, I could not recollect seeing such movements and postures on any ancient Egyptian pictures. At that time I intended to write a treatise on ancient Egyptian dances, but my philological work did not then permit me to carry the idea into effect.

When, however, my daughter Irena became my pupil, it occurred to me that it would be easier to aquaint her with the methods of scientific work than for me to gain expert knowledge of dancing, and for that reason I set her to study the Egyptian dances in the course of seminary work.

My daughter first collected all published material and pictures, and her elder sister Milada copied in ink pictures of dances from reproductions of ancient Egyptian reliefs and pictures made in most diverse ways. In the seminary work we went through every necessary detail, and ascertained some materials empirically.

Thereupon my daughter Irena wrote her treatise, the contents of which appeared to me to be interesting to anyone to whom history of culture is a pleasant source of knowledge and recreation, and I gave permission for its publication. In order to arrive at its goal, it appeared necessary to leave out quite a number of technical details which would

5

merely bore the reader, and to vary the dry scientific style so that he or she might better enjoy it. This part has been carried out by myself, and, confident of its success, I hereby present this our joint work to the public.

Prague, 19th March, 1930.

Dr. František Lexa.

I. THE TREATISE

INTRODUCTION.

Much has been written about the a n c i e n t Egyptian dances.

As far as I can remember, the oldest essay dealing with this subject was written by *J. Gardner Wilkinson* in his book: "M a n n e r s   a n d   c u s t o m s   o f   t h e   a n c i e n t   E g y p - t i a n s", (London, 1837; Part II, pages 328-340). In an abridged form this essay appears in the book by *J. Gardner Wilkinson:* "A   p o p u l a r   a c c o u n t   o f   t h e   a n c i e n t E g y p t i a n s", (new edition I.-II. London, 1874; Part I, pages 133-140).

Credit is due to Wilkinson in the first place for the vast pictorial material he has made accessible. The short essay in Part I, pages 133-140, may be summed up as follows: The dance consisted of a succession of figures in which the performer endeavoured to exhibit a great variety of gestures. Men and women danced at the same time or in separate groups, but the latter were preferred for their superior grace and elegance. Some danced to slow airs, adapted to the style of the movements, others preferred lively steps regulated by an appropriate tune. Sometimes when dancing the women accompanied themselves on lutes or pipes. Men always danced with great spirit, bounding from the ground more in the manner of Europeans than of an Eastern people. Dances were accompanied by music, consisting sometimes of several instruments (harp, lyre, lute, guitar, pipes, tambourine, &c.) at another time by clapping of hands only, or by snapping of fingers; in the street by beating the drum only. Graceful attitudes and gesticulations were features of the

7

general style of ancient Egyptian dancing. Some postures resembled those of our modern ballet, e. g., the pirouette was appreciated by the Egyptians thousands of years ago. Sometimes they danced in pairs holding each other's hands, turning their faces towards each other or averting them. Sometimes men and women performed a solo, marking time with the feet. The quality of the dance obviously depended on the talent and the art of the dancer and on the taste of those for whom it was performed. Comical gestures of clowns were permitted as well, so long as they did not overstep the limits of decency. The dances of the lower classes had a tendency to pantomime, and labourers delighted in grotesqueness and eccentricity more than in grace and elegance.

Women dancers were dressed in long loose robes made of fine transparent material, which permitted of observing the figure and movements of limbs. At times they wore a narrow ornamental girdle. Sometimes the women are represented without any indication of dress and appear to be perfectly nude, but it is difficult to say whether this is not simply an impression caused by the outlines of the dress having been effaced, or if the painter omitted to paint them on account of their transparency.

To banquets and festivals the professional musicians and dancing girls were also invited to entertain the guests by music and dances, which was considered an indispensable condition of good entertainment. In the houses of the rich, slaves were kept, whose duty it was, in addition to other occupations, to divert their masters and their guests with the art of dancing. But it was not customary for a well bred ancient Egyptian to indulge in the dance in public or in private, — that was the privilege of the lower classes. Dancing, however, was a part of education as well as music.

The Egyptians danced also within the temples in honour of their deities, and outside them during religious festivals. This custom was borrowed from them by the Jews, who neither considered it incompatible with the dignity of religion.   *   *
                                                                *

8

This oldest treatise on the Egyptian dancing is quite modest. The author confines himself to facts gathered from ancient Egyptian pictures, and never attempts even to classify the dances.

Note: In a new edition of Wilkinson's work,*) Birch literally reprints Wilkinson's chapter on the dance from the first edition of his book, and supplements it with a paragraph on pictures of dances from the walls of tombs in the Old Empire and with a final remark.

Adolf Erman: "A e g y p t e n u n d a e g y p t i s c h e s L e-b e n i m A l t e r t u m, neu bearbeitet von *Hermann Ranke*" (Tübingen, 1923), writes:

Dancing was not to be omitted from any of the ancient Egyptian festivals, because to the Egyptian it was a natural expression of joy. The farmer, bringing sacrifice to the god Min in Gebtiu at harvest time, always danced. Dancing went on during the festivals held in honour of the great goddesses of joy Hathor and Bastet.

We have little knowledge of these popular dances; at harvest festivals of the Old Empire, men danced having previously put aside their dress except the belt, performing quick movements and holding canes in their hands, clapping them together.

More frequently we meet with dances performed by women of the household, by which they diverted their masters and mistresses. Judging by the old pictures these dances are very quiet and restrained. The dancers followed one after another, hardly lifting their feet from the ground and moving their hands; sometimes other women beat time clapping their hands, at others they were accompanied by airs on harps and pipes.

But in this period already more lively dances are met

---

*) *J. Gardner Wilkinson:* "T h e m a n n e r s a n d c u s t o m s o f t h e a n c i e n t E g y p t i a n s" (new edition revised and corrected by *Samuel Birch*, I.–III. London 1878, Part. I., pages 500–510).

with, which may be compared with our present day ballet. Also pair dancing occurs, and a picture dating from the Sixth Dynasty has been preserved in which girls, dancing with canes ornamented with little gazelle-heads, are divided—as it seems—into fours. More complicated dances, performed by men, occur rarely. One of such dances consisting of three sections has been known from a tomb, dating from the end of the Fourth Dynasty. The dancers, dressed in belts trimmed with long tassels, are facing each other, holding each others' hands and executing the same movements. In the first section they are lifting hands and feet opposite each other; in the second, they are standing on one leg and bending the other at the knee like storks; in the third one they exhibit a back to back position as if they wanted to flee in opposite directions. Each section of this dance bears its particular name, because the Egptians saw certain meanings in them. Such dances are not very far remote from our tableaux vivants. These we encounter in one of the Beni Hassan tombs; in one of them two girls are depicted, one representing a king, the other his defeated enemy. On the other one a girl represents the wind, the two others a bush and grass respectively swayed by the wind. The participating girls are dressed in men's short aprons, the customary dress of women dancers in the Old and Middle Kingdoms showing the body covered as scantily as possible. The dancers wear necklaces, bracelets, rings on their feet and garlands on their heads. The chest is covered with ribbons. Their hair has sometimes been braided into a pigtail, the end of which has been weighted with a ball so as to ensure a graceful line during the dance.

The girl servants diverted their masters and mistresses also with games, neither were acrobatic performers lacking. The span was a known accomplishment to them. One of them, drawn from a Beni Hassan tomb, so controlled her body, that being bent backward in an arch and not touching the ground with her hands, she was in a position to carry a companion on her body. Another one with her head turned downward is being carried by her companion, two others are being whisked about by men, touching the ground only by heels. They are dressed in the customary long robes.

The dancers of the New Kingdom exchanged the men's apron for long transparent linen cloaks, which more revealed than concealed the body, or wore a narrow belt round their hips only. Dances of this period were more refined. Whereas previously the dancers were accompanied by music, now hired women dance at the banquets beating time themselves with tambourines or castagnettes in quick tempo.

✻   ✻
✻

This essay is accompanied by four pictures only (fig. 46, page 175, fig. 120-122, pages 280-282), but in the notes exact references are made to many pictures, which Wilkinson has omitted from his work.

For my part, there is only one objection to this essay. The author in his description considers our picture fig. 32 to be an illustration of three quiet postures instead of three phases of the same movement, and it does not occur to him that this posture—according to the physical law of balance—is altogether impossible. Correct comprehension of this picture would have led the author to a different interpretation of other pictures as well.

A. Wiedemann: Das alte Aegypten (Kulturge-schichtliche Bibliothek, herausgegeben von W. Foy, I. Reihe: Ethnologische Bibliothek 2, Heidelberg, 1920) devotes an independent chapter to the dance (pages 371-375) with two pictures (fig. 73, page 373, and fig. 26 on the attached plates) and four hieroglyphic signs, representing dancing men (page 371).

Although persons of higher standing did not themselves dance for pleasure, dancing was of considerable importance to the Egyptians. As shown by hieroglyphic signs, repre-

11

senting joy and its expression, the Egyptian, when giving way to the feeling of happiness, could not resist bounding and performing other movements, which especially in festive moments certainly were not arbitrary. So for instance on the arrival of the king and other persons of importance such bounds were executed by two men, armed with boomerangs, while three others likewise armed were beating time. At religious processions women danced around the sacred barge naked, or dressed in cloaks open in front, to the accompaniment of music, in order to chase away the demons by their complete or partial nudity. The participation at such ceremonies was rigorously observed and lists of participating temple servants have been preserved.

Also the king or his representative was obliged to dance at harvest festivals in honour of Min, the god of fertility. The often depicted king's haste with the sacrificial gift to the deity cannot be considered as a sacrificial dance. The speed simply demonstrates the zeal with which the king hurried to offer his sacrifice to the god.

Also the religious dances during funerals were of importance to the Egyptians. Women in long robes, playing musical instruments and lashing the air with branches, took part in the procession, while before the tomb a dance was performed for the benefit of the departed soul. Men provided with high caps made of rushes moved about in quiet steps; women clapping hands marked time. Sometimes the movements were livelier, the dancers rotated quickly and raised their feet high. At other times the dancers, conducted by a leading dancer, sped quickly forward bearing sacrificial instruments.

The movements of women dancers were considerably livelier than those of men. They fell in with a festive step, but then thrust about their hands and feet with all their might. Such dances are still customary at funerals in Egypt and in adjacent countries as well. The aim of the dance was not merely to cheer up the soul of the deceased, but also to chase away evil spirits who might harm the dead person,

12

and for that reason the Egyptian, when still alive, often expressed the wish that dances should not fail to be included in burial ceremonies. The model which the dancers participating at funerals were following was the god Bes, who sometimes alone, sometimes with his companions, protected the young Sun from his enemies through dancing. As he was of a dwarfish figure, the Egyptians considered the burial dances especially efficacious if executed by a dwarf.

Also at banquets women danced to entertain the guests. Dressed rather in long than short robes or aprons, sometimes they were completely naked or had a narrow belt round their hips. Often they moved slowly, playing musical instruments, ordinarily in groups of two or more, seldom singly. Men dancers who were conspicuous through physical training, comical postures and movements seldom performed at banquets. With such dances they diverted the public in the streets for tips.

✻　✻
✻

A carefully compiled list of literature dealing with ancient Egyptian dances, which has been attached to this essay, deserves special notice.

Louise Klebs, Die Reliefs des alten Reiches, Die Reliefs und Malereien des mittleren Reiches, Heidelberg, 1915, 1922.

The authoress presents a complete list of all known pictures of dances from the Old and Middle Kingdoms, classifies them historically and describes them briefly.

✻　✻
✻

The classification of the dances evokes my doubts regarding her opinion that slaughtering of cattle in the Old Kingdom was accompanied by dancing in the same manner as in the Middle Kingdom dances were performed to a dying person or to a corpse, lying on the death-bed. Pictures of dancers in the vicinity of such scenes appear to me to be purely accidental.

Historically the classification of ancient Egyptian dances in the way the authoress has carried it out evokes serious doubts, because of its logically erroneous judgment.

Pierre Montet in his book entitled "S c è n e s d e l a v i e p r i v é e d a n s l e s t o m b e a u x é g y p t i e n s d e l'a n c i e n e m p i r e" (Publications de la faculté des lettres de l'Université de Strasbourg, vol. 24, 1925) devotes a chapter to dancing on pages 365–368, the contents of which are as follows: From the fact that women dancers are as a rule depicted in a row under a line of musicians it does not follow that they danced to the accompaniment of music. The musicians are men; since women dancers have too short dresses, the master of the tomb would hardly allow other men to look at them. Women beating time with their hands always accompany women dancers. The vicinity of men musicians and women dancers can be explained by natural association of views by the artist who created the ornaments of the tomb.

In earlier times the dance consisted of a group of women with hands folded above the head, proceeding forward in time, so that one may rather speak of a march than of a dance. Later the movements of the women became more unrestrained; standing on one leg they inclined their bodies backward and lifted the other leg forward. Sometimes they held instruments provided with little gazelles' heads, striking them together and so beating time. Later on more space in the tombs was reserved for pictures of dancing; new dances appear with particular names given to them, which sometimes are written on the pictures.

The reason which M. Montet brings forth for his assumption that dancers were not accompanied by musicians, is not convincing. It is true, that from the pictures originating in the Old Kingdom it cannot be judged whether the

14

dance was accompanied by music or not, but from the pictures of other periods, representing women dancers accompanied by music, one can assume that the same conditions prevailed also in the Old Kingdom, except in the ceremonial funeral dances.

We also know, that nudity was not so rare and so exciting a phenomenon to the ancient Egyptians as it would be to us to-day. That women danced at banquets adorned with jewels and girdles concealing nothing is attested by pictures fig. 13, 45, 48. The dancers wore short skirts not to exhibit their bodies, but in order that their legs should have complete freedom of movement, which would not be possible, if they were dressed in the usual women's dress, the long narrow robe. It is also possible to assume that dances, even in the oldest times, were not confined to the gestures depicted on pictures of tombs of the Old Kingdom. The artists selected these postures either out of incapacity to paint other dancing postures more difficult to draw, requiring quick perception (see fig. 13, 40), or drew the pictures from patterns, or copied old models out of indolence instead of artistically creating new ones.

NATURE OF THE MATERIAL AND
WORKING METHODS.

As allusions to dances in ancient Egyptian literature are very rare, pictures are almost the exclusive source of study of the Egyptian dances.

In present day art the painter is required to depict what he sees in just the way that he sees it, and if he happens to lack a model to give his figure a natural gesture or movement, that is to say a gesture or movement which is not impossible or intolerable, in order to avoid in the spectator the impression of something unnatural. The Egyptian creative artist, however, when drawing a human figure, was bound to observe certain prescriptions not in accordance with present day requirements. He did not draw as he saw, but as the prescription ordered him. Consequently, if the spectator wants to understand the ancient Egyptian paintings, he must know the respective prescriptions to understand what attitude or movement the Egyptian artist intended to illustrate by his work. That is why it is necessary to get acquainted with the important methods of depicting the human body.[1]

I.

When drawing a god, king or a distinguished person in a quiet position, the Egyptian artist had to observe unconditionally these rules: He had to draw the legs up to the

---

[1] The best treatise on drawing the human body is given in *Miroslav Beránek's* work: T h e n e w c o n c e p t i o n o f s p a c e i n t h e a r t o f a n c i e n t E g y p t, Veraikon, vol. VI, 1919—1920 (in Czech).

hips in profile, to put the person's further leg forward and make both feet face the spectator in such a way that the great toes covered the other toes.[2]) The abdomen is shown *en trois quarts* position. The upper part of the body at the back shows the outline of hip, drawn *en face*, the front side shows the outline of chest drawn in profile. The shoulders are drawn *en face* and the arms in full length, turned with their outer sides towards the spectator.[3]) The throat and the head again in profile, but the eyes *en face*.

2.

If the painter illustrated such a figure in movement, he proceeded as if he had a wooden model before him: he bent the toes in the foot, he bent the foot at the ankle, the leg at the knee or the groin, the body at the waist, the fingers on the hand, the hand at the wrist, he bent the head forward or backward, but the outlines of the component parts of the body remained unchanged as on the figure in a quiet position.[4])

3.

When painting persons of lower social classes, such as artisans, workers, servants, &c., the artist was not bound by the prescribed rigorous rules. The figures of common people were drawn in direct profile almost as often as in the pre-

---

[2]) Sometimes the toes are drawn in front of the big toe, turned towards the spectator.

[3]) Sometimes both thumbs are turned upwards the figure having thus two right hands, or downwards, both hands being left; another time the incorrect position of the thumbs causes the figure to show the right hand on the left side and the left hand on the right side.

[4]) In reality it was the artisan who proceeded in this way. An artist, when about to draw the human body in a more difficult moving position, drew the figure according to a model from a perspectively prepared sketch, as a present day artist would do, and then replaced the natural parts in ink by the prescribed parts. Quite a number of such sketches has been preserved. On some of them the replacement is unfinished, evidently because the artist gave up the

scribed way.[5]) Seldom were they drawn *en face*,[6]) very seldom from behind.[7])

4.

As a rule Egyptian painters avoided drawing the human figure from the front or from behind as well as from profile but in the way, that he replaced it by a figure drawn to prescriptions. In fig. 22 and 30 a dancing game is illustrated known as merry-go-round. The youth in front should have been drawn from the back and the one in the rear from the front, but the painter has drawn the bodies of both to prescription, only in fig. 11a he has drawn the youth's feet perspectively.[8])

5.

When the ancient Egyptian painter wanted to illustrate a group of persons facing him, or a file from the side, he dislocated them in such a way that in the picture all persons have been drawn as one behind the other,[9]) or he drew only

---

task of drawing the difficult movements because he was not able to reduce the perspectively prepared sketch to a drawing which would correspond to the prescriptions.

[5]) See fig. 22, 24, 27, 40, 41, 45 (the middle girl), 64 on the left, 65 in the middle, 66—71 and others. The routinist, who was not used to paint from a model, when drawing a human figure in profile, turned over the front half of the figure, made to prescription, on to the back half; see fig. 35, the figure of the clapping girl; fig. 5, the seated men fig. 54.

[6]) See fig. 64. Here and in fig. 49 the upper part of the body has been drawn *en face*, but the lower part, fig. 49, is drawn according to prescription and in fig. 46 from profile. Drawings of the human body *en face* are found on prehistoric pictures; see fig. 1, 2.

[7]) See fig. 22 on the right. See *J. G. Wilkinson:* "M a n n e r s a n d c u s t o m s o f t h e a n c i e n t E g y p t i a n s", Ist edition part III., page 135, fig. 354, fig. 2, where the weaver sitting at the loom is drawn from behind.

[8]) How thoughtlessly the painters worked is evident in fig. 11a, where the young man in the rear is drawn standing between the reclining partners instead of being put behind them, and in fig. 30, where the women suspended in a recumbent position are drawn in front of the men instead of between them.

[9]) Fig. 59.

the person standing nearest to him, and he marked the others only in outlines.[10]) In fig. 38 the painter used both these methods conjointly. The seven women in the picture are grouped in this configuration:

The manner in which the clapping women are drawn makes their arms impossibly long, but the painter reached his aim: he persuaded us that the picture represents a file of three women.

6.

When illustrating a movement the Egyptian could depict either one characteristic momentary position of the body, in the manner of the present day artist,[11]) or he could draw various phases as found in textbooks on gymnastics. The first method is generally used, seldom the other.[12])

We thus come to this conclusion:

1. A figure drawn to prescription can represent a figure turned toward the spectator, facing him fully or partially, showing either a dorsal or lateral position.

2. A figure or a group of figures may represent a quiet posture or a fraction of the movement.

*   *
*

N o t e : The reproductions of ancient Egyptian pictures which have so far been published are as a rule not exact. This fact can be explained in this way, that the artist who has to copy hundreds of pictures in one tomb only is confined as to the time at his disposal and cannot bestow enough care upon his drawings. That also explains why on reproductions of some pictures, made by various artists, differences of details can be detected; as the reader will see in fig. 43,

---

[10]) Fig. 54.
[11]) See for instance the youth jumping on fig. 36, 37, the woman dancer forming the bridge on fig. 40.
[12]) See fig. 16—21, 26, 31, 32.

and 44, illustrating dances from the tomb of Haremhab, Fig. 43 is redrawn from Bouriant's treatise, fig. 44 from Wilkinson's book. These differences, which however seldom vary so considerably as in this case, are due to the original being sometimes unclear or damaged. Heliographic reproductions from the original are, with regard to details, still less clear, as the reader could ascertain on the heliographic reproductions of the picture included in *W. Wreszcinski's* book, "Atlas zur altägyptischen Kulturgeschichte", pl. 251. We have to be satisfied with the fact that these differences of detail are unimportant for our purposes.

CLASSIFICATION OF THE ANCIENT EGYPTIAN DANCES.

The preserved ancient Egyptian pictures of dances give us sufficient material for the classification of ancient Egyptian dances according to the intrinsic contents into groups, each of which we shall treat separately.

I. THE PURELY MOVEMENTAL DANCE.

Originally the dance was a simple outburst of superfluous energy accumulated in a reposing man who was not accustomed to inactivity. Both the dancer and the casual onlooker derived joy from the movement, the rythm of which served the purpose of economising energy, putting off the fatigue and prolonging the possibility of the movement. The subconscious and undisciplined movements of the dancer turned into conscious and disciplined ones, as soon as the spectators began to be interested in the dance, and accompanied it with clapping of hands and rythmical cries. Also the endeavour to excel over other women and men dancers surely contributed to the evolution of the movemental dance, lacking other intrinsic bases. In this group may be entered the dances depicted in fig. 1, 2, dating from prehistoric times, and those in fig. 39, 49, 51, from later times. The coincidence of postures of the Egyptian women and men dancers in the ritual funeral dances fig. 4, 5, 8, 23, 74 with the postures of the dancers on the prehistoric vessels fig. 1, 2, are a new proof of the conservatism of religious and funeral customs of ancient Egypt.

21

II. THE GYMNASTIC DANCE.

The endeavour to excel over others induces some of the dancers to refine the delicacy and taste of movements, some others to choose more difficult and more strenuous movements such as not everyone is capable of performing, because they require great physical elasticity and long training. Such gymnastic or acrobatic dances were depicted by the ancient Egyptian painters in the following pictures:

In picture 10 we see a beautiful dancing movement. The woman dancer is standing on one leg, the other one is lifted up very high. Her trunk is inclined backward and the arms are stretched out in a parallel position to the raised leg. It is almost a split, made the more difficult because it is being executed at a perpendicular level and the upraised leg lacks any support. Is it only a sudden movement from which the dancer will return to the upright position, or is it a preparation for a long step forward? In fig. 41 on the left we see two women in almost impossible inclines from the point of view of physical balance; probably the painter has illustrated momentary gestures, from which the girls will go over to form a span.

That the span was a favoured dancing posture can be ascertained from the preserved reproductions (fig. 24, 40, 41) and from a statue (fig. 25). Whereas the spans in fig. 40, 41 are excellently arched, the span in fig. 24 is only slightly so, and on the statue fig. 25 it is quite flat, so that here it is difficult to imagine a return to an upright position. The dancer may, of course, approach her hands to her feet and return into an arched span position, or by distancing her hands and feet she would be able to come into a recumbent position or by moving her hands and feet to walk on all-fours.

From the artist's point of view the picture reproduced in fig. 40 is especially valuable, because he drew the girl in the moment just before she completed the span.

In fig. 35 the girls' initial position was a facial prostration. Leaning with hands on the ground and arching their bodies, they lift the upper part of their bodies inclining the heads and simultaneously lifting and bending the legs, trying to touch their heads with them.

Grotesque is the dancer's performance in fig. 31 on the right. Either she is jumping to a slight height, making use of the moment when her centre of gravity is rising and falling to draw quickly her legs to the body and then to stretch them out again, so that the spectator gains a false impression that the upper part of the girl's body remains still and that only the legs are alternatively drawn under and stretched out, or that she rebounds and springs forward all the time.

The girl marked "d" in fig. 31 does not probably belong to the group in this picture, being the only one in a long woman's robe. If this single posture induced the painter to illustrate her action, it appears that she was moving forward with an almost imperceptible motion of the legs, remaining upright all the time.

It was no easy task to jump rhythmically with upright body and almost imperceptible rebounds as illustrated in fig. 36 and 37, the movement being enlivened in fig. 36 by a woman and in fig. 37 by a man, who by gestures of feet and hands try to encourage the jumping boy to a more perfect performance.

It is a difficult question as to where is the boundary between an acrobatic dance and pure acrobatics. In fig. 32 the artist has caught three movements of a complicated performance of two women dancers. The complete course of this performance may be imagined thus:

Two girls of approximately equal height and strength take up a position with legs astride, one behind the other. The first one arches her body almost to span and embraces her companion around the waist. The other girl somewhat inclines her body and grasps the first one also around the waist. Thus the second girl straightens herself up and lifts the first one in such a way that the latter keeping her head

23

downwards, passes her legs round the head of her mate and bends them forward.

The second girl inclines to such an extent that the legs of the first dancer touch the ground and thus the original position is formed again, in which the places and tasks of both girls are interchanged. By sufficient training the girls may attain such a proficiency, that they will execute whole series of such movements in exact rythm.

Acrobatic dances of ancient Egypt have been described by a young man of Syracuse, who visited Memphis at the end of the fourth century B. C. Having been invited by a rich Egyptian to a banquet, he describes the dances with which the host entertained his guests. The respective part of the letter runs in English translation as follows:[13])

Suddenly they disappeared and in their place came forward a group of dancers, who jumped about in all directions, gathered together again, climbed one on top of the other with an incredible dexterity, mounting on the shoulders and the heads, forming pyramids, reaching to the ceiling of the hall, then descended suddenly one after the other to perform new jumps and admirable *saltomortales*. Being in constant motion, now they danced on their hands, now they gathered in pairs, one turning his head down between the legs of his mate, then they lifted themselves mutually and returned to the original position, each of them alternatively being lifted and upon falling lifted his partner up.

I think that the reader will recognise without any difficulty in the description of the acrobatic pair dances, the same dance which is depicted in fig. 32 and which is described above. The words "they gathered in pairs, climbed one on top of the other with incredible dexterity mounting on the shoulders and heads..." said at the beginning of the previous paragraph of the letter, are a description of

[13]) According to a German translation published by *Fritz Weege* in his book "Der Tanz in der Antike", pp. 28—29, without giving his authority.

24

fig. 29, which the author entitled by the word "heaven".

It is obvious that the Syracusan speaks about dancers, but he describes among the dances also purely acrobatic performances. I was rather embarrassed, whether to classify the performance of the girls' pair in fig. 32 among dances. The performance of the boys in fig. 29 I do not take for a dance at all, whereas our Syracusan traveller is not preoccupied with this question. Judging by the commencement of the letter, all the performances described were accompanied by music and may have been carried out rhytmically. To the Syracusan every movement accompanied by music was a dance.

III. THE IMITATIVE DANCE

Dancers of all nations and of all times imitate movements of animals. Among the primitive nations, to which the ancient Egyptians do not belong—the aim of these dances, imitating movements of animals and nature's phenomena, is to attract the animals or to evoke a certain natural phenomenon. The African natives perform an ostrich dance before they start for an ostrich hunt, believing that through these dances they will attract the ostriches. The medicine men attempt through their dance to bring about rain, resulting in abundant harvests, &c. Among advanced nations, the imitative dance amuses the spectator either through its grotesqueness or by the comparison to what degree men or women dancers will succeed in imitating what they endeavour to copy.

So far there is not even one single ancient Egyptian picture aiming to illustrate a dance imitating animal movements; from this, however, we cannot judge that the ancient Egyptians were not acquainted with them. Correlation of the ideas of animal movement and dances testify to the contrary. So for instance it had been written about the king Ahmes Nebpehtire on a stone slab, which used to stand in the temple of Amon in Karnak: "His splendour is (reflected) in the countenances of men as the splendour of Atum[14]) on the eastern skies, when the ostrich dances in the desert."[15])

A teacher admonishing a pupil to industry and obedience says to him: "Devote your heart to obey what I am telling you and you will find that it is useful. Kaeri[16]) also learns to dance, a horse gets tamed, a wild pidgeon is put into the pidgeon hole to become tame, a falcon has his wings tied."[17])

The imitation of movements of a natural phenomenon in dancing is illustrated by the scene "*b*" in fig. 28. In order to facilitate its comprehension, the painter marked it with the word "Wind". This inscription and the illustration permit us to imagine what the complete dance looked like. The narrow junction of the heterogenous scenes a) and b) shows that the painter was economising in space. For that reason he drew the girl's erect figure so closely to the other girls that her outstretched arms are above them. In reality the girl representing the wind was standing at a distance from the two other girls, and by thrusting out her arms, illustrated gusts of wind. The two girls then illustrated swaying plants, rushes, canes, &c. by their bending.

This dance also leads to the conclusion that the Egyptians were acquainted with animal dances, because the imitation of a plant movement is surely younger than that of the animals. Is it really a mere accident that the dancers' bodies in the slightly arched span in fig. 24 reveal a posture of greyhounds?

IV. THE PAIR DANCE.

Pair dancing, in the sense as used to-day, was not known to the Egyptians at all; so far no single ancient Egyptian

---

[14]) Atum is the god of the sun; here he represents the sunrise.
[15]) "Urkunden des ägyptischen Altertums" IV., p. 19, 9—10.
[16]) The word "kaëri" is not of Egyptian origin; it denotes some quadruped.
[17]) From the hieratic papyri Anastasi III, 3/9—4/4 = Anastasi V, 8/I—9/I (Select papyri in the Hieratic Character).

picture has been found illustrating a man and woman dancing and embracing each other, or at least holding each other's hands. The pairs in ancient Egypt were formed either by two men or two women.

From the Vth Dynasty we know a group of girls dancing in pairs (fig. 13); they hold their hands, facing each other and standing on one leg they lift the other one which is bent forward at the knee so that their toes meet. It is not clear as to what preceded this position and in what way the dance went on; it is possible that in fig. 15 on the left some other posture of the same pair dance may be illustrated, whereas what we find on the right of the same picture is not a dancing pair, but a dancing master training a girl.

The position of the pair dance in fig. 16–21 showes how seriously the Egyptians of the Old Kingdom took the art of dancing. There are six of them and each bears its own name; it is a pity that it is not possible to ascertain the exact meaning of these wordings, because the words admit of several interpretations; for instance the inscription of the first group fig. 16 may express the idea of "longing", the second group fig. 17 "emancipation", the third group fig. 18 "the gold which is to be fetched", (or robbed), the fourth group fig. 19 "secret abduction", the fifth group fig. 20 "depression", the sixth group fig. 21, robbing (or fetching) a beauty; but there may be other meanings as well.

What was the psychological connection of these appellations with the dancing postures? The pictures show us merely that the two dancers executed symmetrical movements, and that they were constantly keeping to the level perpendicular to the direction from the point of view of the spectator.

In and out movements followed one upon another, now with arms slightly lowered, then again with arms slightly bent. To charm the spectators by perfect symmetry of movements was probably the chief aim of this dance. Fig. 55 reveals to us that the New Kingdom Egyptians enjoyed the symmetrical dance as much as their ancestors of the Old

27

Kingdom did. Here, however, the dancers do not hold hands, but clench their fists, touching each other with their thumbs only. Symmetrical was, without a doubt, also the dance of the girls with the wooden clappers in fig. 57; just because they did not hold their hands, they had more freedom of movement than their colleagues in the preceding pictures.

In fig. 33 and 34 we see four pairs of dancing women. Three pairs are facing each other, in the second pair, however, one woman is turning her back to her partner; this leads to the conclusion that in this pair dance the dancers rotated. Perhaps it is unnecessary to draw the reader's attention to the hard movements of the women in this picture in comparison to the movements illustrated in all other pictures. Did the artist want to draw a cartoon of a dance, with clumsy movements and postures, in order to evoke hilarity in the spectator, who was accustomed to refined and graceful movements of women dancers? Did the women in this dance followed a certain idea?

It would be difficult to decide whether the dance of the two women in fig. 39 was in some sort correlated, or whether each dancer performed the dance independently of her partner.

The rest of the pair dances which we find in our pictures contain an intrinsic idea, and we shall take them into consideration elsewhere.

V. THE GROUP DANCE.

If by group dancing we mean dances lacking an intrinsic idea, in which all performers execute different movements, which however are organically interconnected, we may in the first place mark as such a so-called merry-go-round of the two boys and girls in fig. 30 and a merry-go-round of the six boys in fig. 22, provided that merry-go-round can be taken for a dance at all.

An obvious group dance is represented in fig. 38, in which four dancers are seen divided in pairs, advancing in a dancing step towards each other, the three women in the background beating time by clapping of hands. What was the further proceeding when they met is, however, a question which cannot be answered.

In fig. 51 a group of five dancers is represented, every one performing different movements. It appears, however, that these movements are independent of each other; every one is dancing without taking heed of the others, only the time-measure is the link which connects their dancing.

With regard to fig. 33 it is different. Between the two grown-up dancers, one of whom is playing a lute and the other a double pipe, a small girl is dancing making probably use of castagnettes. Whereas the movements of the two grown-up women were restricted by the musical instruments, the girl had complete freedom of movements and her dance surely was much more vivacious than that of her older companions, who provided only a moderately mobile medium for her.

In fig. 57 eight women dancers, standing in two ranks of four, are performing moderate dance movements and two lively dancing girls are accompanying with rhytmical strokes on little drums with wooden clappers. Here again the moderate movements of the grown updancers pursued the same goal as those in the previous dance.

If by group dancing in a wider sense of the word we mean dances of persons performing identical movements, then we have to classify as such also the ritual funeral dances, which originally were not funeral dances at all but became so later on account of their antiquity. Ranks of dancers executing identical movements impressed the spectator by the repetition of the element in question in the same way as a graphic or sculptural ornament. (Fig. 34, 41, 59, 75, 76.) [18])

---

[18]) Individual figures (fig. 5—12, 23, 74) are also taken out of rows of figures represented in the same attitude.

VI. THE WAR DANCE.

Fig. 60 and 61 form parts of two larger pictures, in which the artist drew scenes from contemporary life. In the period of the New Kingdom, from which time the two pictures originate, the Egyptians kept a mercenary army on the whole, in which the black Mazioi, the Hamitic Lybians, the Semitic Pedtiu and the Shardans originating from the Mediterranean islands are represented. In the soldiers depicted in fig. 60 it is not difficult to recognise coloured men; the soldiers in fig. 61 are of Lybian origin.

War dances were a current recreation of resting troops. In what degree the national character of the troops has been reflected in them, can be seen by comparison of the two pictures.

The coloured men's dance is a wild mixture of undisciplined movements, accompanied by deafening shouts. The big drum, still used by some African negro tribes, is trying to stifle the shouts by its rhythmical sound and to guide the dancers' movements.

The Lybian soldiers beat time by striking curved pieces of wood (boomerang?) together and their comrades, also provided with curved pieces of wood, are performing a dance, which is probably a representation of a duel; that at least is the posture of the soldier on the left, who is giving an impression of a pretended attack, whereas the posture of his mate is that of defence in retreat.

VII. THE DRAMATIC DANCE.

In picture 28a the participating girls exhibit postures well known from historical pictures; the kneeling girl represents a defeated enemy king, the standing girl an Egyptian king, who with his left hand is holding the enemy prince by the hair and in his right hand holds a war club to smash the head of the defeated enemy. The oldest historical picture of this kind has been known from the palette, used for the preparation of eye-paints for the Egyptian king Narmer, who ends the succession of the prehistoric kings and is followed to the throne by king Menes, with whom the succession of historical kings commences. The picture bears the inscription "under the feet" this being an abbreviation of a sentence, which occurs as a rule in inscriptions supplementing the above-mentioned historical pictures, viz. "all foreign people lie under your feet". From this the conclusion is drawn that our picture does not represent a dancing scene but a *tableau vivant*.

I think that this assumption is not quite justified. The historical picture represents the decisive moment of the king's fight with the enemy. One can imagine the course of the whole action from beginning to end. The enemy prince encounters the Egyptian king; in the following duel the prince succumbs, throws his weapon away and takes to flight; the king pursues him and the prince, seeing that it is impossible for him to escape, falls on his knees and asks for pardon; the king grasps his hair with the left hand and with the club in his right hand smashes his head; the prince falls at his feet dead.

The artist could not have represented the whole action in one picture, but in the historical picture as well as in ours he selects the decisive scene, representing the whole action in the same manner, as in other pictures he draws one moment of the action only, be it a dance, hunting, artisan's work, audience of foreign nations, bringing gifts to the king, or a battle scene. It never occurred to anyone yet to consider these scenes as *tableaux vivants* arranged as a spectacle for the owner of the tomb during his earthly life.

Remarkable is the difference between the war dance of the soldiers in fig. 61 and the dramatic dance here described. The soldiers dance with pieces of wood, which probably are real weapons (boomerangs?) or their imitations; but the dancer in fig. 28a representing a king is executing an adapted movement without a club in her hand with which to smash the opponent's head. That is the reason why I con-

31

sider the scene indicated to be a dancing scene. Were it to represent a tableau, there would be no reason why the dancer representing the king should lack a club in her hand.

VIII. THE LYRICAL DANCE.

The fact that the Egyptians knew also lyrical dances can be gathered from the description of the banquet given by the rich Egyptian of Memphis, the author of which is a Greek from Syracuse. One part of the description has been quoted above, when I dealt with the gymnastic dance. The respective part of the letter runs as follows.[18a]

"Now I caught sight of a troop of musicians, coming with various musical instruments in their hands, in which I recognised harps, guitars, lyres, simple and double pipes, tambourines and cymbals. We were overwhelmed constantly by songs which were most cordially applauded by the audience. Then, at a given sign, the middle of the hall was taken by a man and a girl dancer, who were provided with clappers. These were made out of two small pieces of wood round and concave, located in the palms, and gave rhythm to the dancing steps when suddenly knocked together. These two dancers danced separately or together in harmonious configurations, mixed with pirouettes, soon parting and again approaching each other, the young dancer running after his mate and following her with expressions of tender desire, while she fled from him constantly, rotating and pirouetting, as if refusing his endeavours after amorous approach. This performance was done lightly and energetically in harmonious postures, and seemed to me exceedingly entertaining."

If we look at our pictures of ancient Egyptian dances, we will find three of them which remind us somewhat of the dance alluded to.

In fig. 14 three dancers are represented; one in a quiet

[18a]) according to a German translation; see note 13, page 24.

posture is dressed in the customary women's dress. The remaining two are in men's skirts, but — unusual as it is — each of them in a different one, in order that the spectator might distinguish clearly one from the other. Both keep the same posture indicative of addressing the girl, who is quietly standing before them. Do not the girls dressed as men represent two rivals competing for the girl's favour?

In fig. 45 the middle girl exhibits a gesture expressing a humble request, whereas the girl standing before her is erect, her gesture seems to express indecision as to whether to grant the request or to refuse it.

In fig. 50 the girl standing in the middle is turning her body to the right towards the girl playing the harp, her head however, is turned to the left towards the girl playing the lute; she has no musical instrument and the movement of her arms also seems to express indecision; again, are not the two musicians competing with music and song for the favour of their companion?

IX. THE GROTESQUE DANCE.

When the caravan leader Herkhuf was returning to Egypt from an expedition, on which he had been sent by king Pepi Neferkare of the VI. Dynasty, he sent a message to the king, telling him that he was successful and brought rich booty for his master. The king answered him in a letter, the contents of which Herkhuf had engraved on the wall of his tomb, the translation of which runs as follows:[19])

"On the 15th day of the third month of inundation in the second year, by the King's order to his only friend, master of the rites, leader of caravans, Herkhuf: I took note of the contents of your letter, which you wrote to the King in his palace to announce that you have happily returned

---

[19]) The best hieroglyphic text edited: *Kurt Sethe,* U r k u n d e d e s a l t e n R e i c h e s, page 128 a. f., translation *Adolf Erman,* D e r B r i e f d e s K ö n i g N e f r-k e'r e in Zeitschrift für die ägyptische Sprache und Altertumskunde XXXI, 1893, page 65 a. f.

from Amaam with the army that accompanied you.

"You have said in your letter that you were bringing great nice gifts of all sorts, which Hathor the mistress of Amaam had given to the spirit of King Neferkare, of Upper and Lower Egypt, may he live for ever and ever!

"Further you have said in this letter that you were bringing along a dwarf of divine dances from the Land of the Spirits, similar to the one who had been brought by the custodian of the divine treasure Bawerded from Punt, in the reign of King Asosi. You have told My Grace, that it never happened before that such a dwarf was brought by anyone who had made a journey to Amaam.

"Be always aware that you are to do what is the wish and what is approved by your Master. Whether awake, or asleep, take care of what is to be done, as wishes, approves, and has been ordered by your Lord. My Grace will fulfil your numerous important wishes, to benefit also your (son and) grandson for ever, so that all people who will have heard, what My Grace has done for you, will say: Nothing is equal to that, what has been received by his only friend Herkhuf, when he returned from Amaam and executed that which he had to do, as was the king's wish, as approved by him and as ordered by his Master.

"Sail immediately on the river to the king's palace. Speed up, and bring with you that dwarf whom you brought from the Land of Spirits, may he live, be in good health and fresh to dance divine dances to cheer the heart of Neferkare the King of Upper and Lower Egypt, may he live for ever!

"When he embarks with you on board ship, see that proper men are with him on both sides of the ship, taking care of him, lest he should fall into the water. See that proper men sleep with him in his tent, and ten times in the night make inspection. My Grace longs to see the dwarf more than the presents of Sinai and Punt. When you have landed at the palace, see that the dwarf is with you in good health, alive and fresh, and My Grace will do for you more

than was done for the custodian of the divine treasure, Bawerded, in the time of King Asosi, because to see this dwarf
is the most ardent desire of My Grace."

From this letter of king Neferkare — at that time a boy
of 10 — it is obvious what a rare treat for the king were
the divine dwarf dances. We are not to attribute the King's
predilection to his youth. What importance was attached
to dwarf dances at that time, we gather from the fact that
in the time of King Neferkare knowledge was preserved not
only about the dwarf, who had been presented some 350
years ago to King Asosi, but also about the man who
brought him to the King at that time.

Kings of the earliest historical periods had their dwarfs
buried in the vicinity of their tombs, as witnessed by the
tomb stelae, of which several have been found. A statue
of a dwarf, carved out of limestone in the Vth Dynasty,
which is now in the possession of the Cairo Museum, be-
longs to the most perfect creations of ancient Egyptian
art.[20])

A companion of the King's spirit, wanting to induce
the boatman in the heavenly meadows to ferry the king's
spirit to the other world, passes him for the dwarf dancer
of Ra, who cheers the god's heart before his great throne.[21])

There has not been found, so far, on the ancient Egyptian pictures a single dwarf dancing, but there are thousands of statuettes, reliefs and pictures of the god Bes, who
frightens away evil spirits by his dance, which have been
preserved. I have chosen two of them (fig. 64, 65).

The effectiveness of the dwarf dances surely consisted
in comical mimics with their clumsy movements.

Although we know relatively numerous pictures of
dwarfs, originating in the Old Kingdom,[22]) they were not

---

[20]) See *Erman-Ranke,* A e g y p t e n u n d ä g y p t i s c h e s L e-
b e n i m A l t e r t u m, Tübingen, 1923, pl. 10, fig. 3.
[21]) Pyramid texts §§ 1168—1192.
[22]) See *Klebs,* D i e R e l i e f s d e s a l t e n R e i c h e s, page
32—33.

so many as to satisfy all who wanted to see the dwarf dances, and for this reason the normally grown-up dancers imitated dwarf dances; so for instance in the reproduction fig. 59 it has been remarked that dwarf dances are being performed; we see, however, that the dancers are regularly grown-up people of the same height as the other contemporaries.

X. THE FUNERAL DANCE.

In the pictures of the ancient Egyptian funeral dances we can distinguish three kinds of dances according to their inner idea: first of all the ritual dances, forming a component part of the funeral rites, then the assumed expression of grief by persons participating at the funerals, and ultimately secular dances performed to entertain the spirit of the deceased.

The most important was the ritual funeral dance. Originally it was a secular dance, held in special esteem on account of its antiquity. We find it already in the prehistoric pictures fig. 1. 2., and in the historical era we constantly meet with it: It is always performed by several men and women dancers, who are accompanied by mates, clapping their hands rhytmically. The women or men move erect with a free dancing step, keeping their hands raised above their heads, as illustrated in fig. 4, which is a reproduction of a whole dancing scene; for the sake of comparison individual figures have been excerpted out of similar dancing scenes, fig. 5, 8 from the Old Kingdom, fig. 23 from the Middle Kingdom, and fig. 74 from the Saïtic period. Other postures of such dances are revealed to us in fig. 3, 7, 11 on the left, originating from the Old Kingdom and fig. 75, 76 from the Saïtic period.

This dance has been known from numerous pictures[23])

---

[23]) A part of these pictures is reproduced in this book either in full, or in part. I know further pictures representing ritual dances: R. *Lepsius*, Denkmäler aus Ägypten und Äthiopien, Berlin, 1849—1856, section II, pl. 14 (six men from the tomb

of the Old Kingdom; as to the Middle Kingdom, from two pictures only, viz. the tombs of the princes Bakti and Kheti in Beni Hassan.[24]) In the new Kingdom it has disappeared, as it seems, completely — at least no picture has been known, emanating from this era; in the Saïtic period it was revived with many other forgotten ancient customs.

From the beginning of the Middle Kingdom the dwarf dance also becomes a funeral ritual dance through the same psychological process as the previous dance, although in the Old Kingdom it was a grotesque secular dance.

The king Senwosret Kheperkare[25]) when summoning to his court Sinuhet, who in his youth fled to Syria, sends him a letter, in which he depicts the honours awaiting him at his court as long as he lives, and the funeral honours to be conferred upon him after his death, which concludes with this words:[26]) "You will be placed under a canopy, bulls will draw you, musicians will precede you and a dwarf

---

No. 6. at Gizeh), pl. 41 fifteen dancers preserved from the tomb No 41 at Gizeh), pl. 53 (four men from the tomb No. 16 at Gizeh), pl. 61a (thirteen men from the tomb No. 16 at Sakkara), pl. 109 (eight men from the tomb No. 2 at Zawiet el Meitin); *N. de G. Davies,* T h e r o c k t o m b s o f S h e i k h S a i d, pl. X. (five women in men's skirts), *L. Klebs,* D i e R e l i e f s d e s a l t e n R e i c h e s, p. 40, fig. 26, according to *Holwerda-Boeser,* B e s c h r e i b u n g d e r ä g y p t i s c h e n S a m m l u n g d e s N i e d e r l ä n d i s c h e n R e i c h s m u s e u m s d e r A l t e r t ü m e r i n L e i d e n I, D e n k m ä l e r d e s a l t e n R e i c h e s, pl. XI. (Preserved have been two women dancers in men's skirts and behind them a standing, clapping girl.)

[24]) *Percy E. Newberry,* B e n i H a s a n II, London, 1894, tab. VII (six women dancers in men's garments, in front of them four clapping women in women's garments), pl. XIII (six women dancers in men's garments and in front of them three clapping women in women's garments), pl. XVII (three dancing and in front of them three clapping men in normal dress).

[25]) King Senwosret I, the second king of the XII Dynasty, who reigned from 1980—1935 B. C.

[26]) The hieratic text with a hieroglyphic transcription published by *Alan H. Gardiner,* D i e E r z ä h l u n g d e s S i n u h e u n d d i e H i r t e n g e s c h i c h t e, Leipzig, 1909.

dance will be performed before the door of your tomb; sacrificial prayers will be said for you and cattle will be slain at your offering table."

This dwarf dance has been depicted in the tomb of Sinuhet's contemporary, the vizier Antefoker.[27] Four well grown men, dressed in the manner of dwarf dancers in fig. 59, are dancing here, the difference being that their right hands are slightly bent and stretched forward, whereas their left hands hang freely along the body; they are called "dwarfs".

Two such men drawn in a quiet posture and equally called dwarfs are also found in the tombs of Rekhmire[28] and Paheri;[29] the same we find in the tomb of Sebeknakht and Sehetebyebre,[30] where the dancers differ from those in our picture 57 only by a somewhat different position of their hands.

Wrongly marked is the pair dance in fig. 55 (and also that of Paheri's tomb[31]) as a dwarf dance. The Egyptians of the New Kingdom knew perfectly well that the dwarf dance was a ritual religious dance already in the early times, and the pair dance was known to them from tombs of the Old Kingdom (fig. 16, 21); from the psychological point of view, therefore, it is explicable why they connected the pair dance of the Old Kingdom with the name of the dwarf dance. This name suggests that also the pair dance became a ritual funeral dance in the New Kingdom.

---

[27] *N. de G. Davies,* The tomb of Antefoker, vizier of Sesostris I, pl. XXII.

[28] *Ph. Virey,* Le tombeau de Rekhmara, pl. XXVI.

[29] *I. J. Tylor* and *F. Ll. Griffith,* The tomb of Paheri, pl. V.

[30] See *A. Moret,* Mystères égyptiens, Paris, 1923, fig. 43, page 257 (after *I. J. Tylor,* Tomb of Sebeknakht, pl. IV.), fig. 13, page 49 (after *I. E. Quibell,* Rameseum, pl. IX.).

[31] *I. J. Tylor* and *F. Ll. Griffith,* The tomb of Paheri, tab. V.; the dancers are found in the same position as in fig. 53, but the hands, which in fig. 53 meet, in the picture of Paheri's tomb are raised up a bit and drawn to the body, so that they do not meet.

The ancient Egyptian expressions of grief were restricted to certain postures and gestures, which the reader will find in fig. 66, 71. It is natural that these movements were adapted and executed rhytmically, as can be seen from the two women on the left in fig. 66, from the two women in the centre of the same picture, and from all the eight persons in fig. 72. Thus the funeral dance originated out of the natural expression of grief, which was not performed at funerals by trained men and women dancers, but by all persons participating, perhaps after training rehearsed by some men and women to whom dancing was a profession.

According to one[32]) ancient Egyptian point of view regarding life after death, the spirit of the deceased lived after death in his tomb exactly as he used during his life on earth, feeling the same joys, sorrows and longings which he felt during his earthly life. In the pyramid of king Pepi Neferkare, one part of a destroyed text has been preserved which runs as follows: "It is being danced to you by the keepers, it is being sung to you by ..."[33]) It is not surprising, therefore, that the same men and women dancers, who danced for him during his life in his house, performed secular dances before the tomb for his entertainment, which he liked best when alive. That is the reason why the ancient Egyptian had them depicted upon the wall of his tomb, believing that the persons depicted, upon hearing the magic spell, would turn into real living persons and attend to the necessities and amusements of their masters. To this belief we owe not only that the majority of pictures illustrating dances have been revealed to us, but as a matter of fact all the phenomena regarding the ancient Egyptian cultural life.

---

[32]) According to other old Egyptian opinions, the spirit of the deceased lived in Osiris's realm of spirits, or in the heavenly medows, or became a star, moving on the skies, or lived in the company of the god Ra.

[33]) Pyramid texts § 1947.

XI. THE RELIGIOUS DANCE.

The dance in ancient Egypt was a component part of the religious service, as was the case with the rest of the ancient nations. The ancient gods possessed all the human qualities, and it was no wonder that they looked with pleasure on nice dances. Ani in his teaching says:

"Song, dance and frankincense are the meals for the god,
Acceptance of worship is his privilege.
Act so that the god's name be hallowed."[34]

In the ritual of the goddess Mut we read: "The towns of Pe, Dep and ......all wreathed with vines are dancing for you".[35]

In the Dendera temple of the goddess Hathor we read:
"We beat the drum to her spirit,
we dance to her Grace,
we raise her image up to the heavenly skies;
She is the lady of sistrum, Mistress of jingling necklaces;"

or: "She is the lady of cheers, mistress of dance,
the lady of sistrum, the mistress of song,
the lady of dance, the mistress of wreath making,
the lady of beauty, the mistress of skipping."

or: "When both her eyes open — the sun and the moon —
our hearts rejoice, seeing the light.
She is the lady of dance wreaths,
the lady of intoxication,
we dance to none, we cheer none,
but her spirit."[36]

---

[34] *F. Lexa*, Enseignements moraux généraux des anciens Égyptiens, tome troisième. Enseignement d'Ani et d'Amenemopet, Praha, 1929, pp. 97, IV. 8—10.
[35] Hieratische Papyrus aus den königlichen Museen zu Berlin, I. Pap. 3053, 18/3—4.
[36] *A. Mariette*, Denderah, III. 60 e—h.

It is not the dances in fig. 56 and 58 which are meant thereby, in which we see a group of women either completely nude, or dressed in broad cloaks opened in front, who march in the procession before the shrine containing the god and who with their nudity, beating of drums, and waving of branches chase away evil spirits, who with hostile intentions obstruct the procession.

In both pictures above mentioned the women accompanying the shrine are Egyptians, whereas in the dancing group permanently employed by the Illahun temple of King Senwosret Kheperkare of the XII Dynasty, there were five Asiatic dancers and two negro women dancers[37]) whose dances pursued another goal.

According to Ani's teaching, frankincense was burnt and dances and songs performed in honour of the god; consequently the dance was a component part of the religious service; we have not, however, any record of what these dances were like. But as also the dwarf dancer, who had been brought for king Pepi Neferkare, performed divine dances,[38]) we may presume that the dances ordained for the worship of a god did not differ from those performed for the king's entertainment, — for the Egyptian king was also a god[39]) — and for other eminent persons.

There are few records concerning ancient Egyptian mysteries. We know that these were of two kinds. Some of them were accessible to a few persons only, the others were entirely public, with masses of spectators actively participating in them.

So during the great mysteries of Osiris in Abydos during the reign of the XII Dynasty, of which we learn from a stela of the Chief Keeper of the treasure, Ikher-

---

[37]) See page 66, C.

[38]) See page 30.

[39]) Following the name of a god in the Egyptian texts there is as a rule an attribute "great god"; following the name of an Egyptian king the attribute "good and beautiful god"; the Egyptian king becomes a great god only after his death.

nofret, whom King Senwosret III appointed his representative in these mysteries, battles were fought in which enemies of Osiris were defeated. No realistically expressed battles come in question here, but merely battles adapted in the same manner as in the battle scene of Memphitic mysteries at the erection of the holy column Zed, about which we learn from the tomb of Kheruf of the XVIII Dynasty, where only 15 persons participated.[40]) Of course it is not out of the question that some of the persons participating played their parts too passionately, and treated their mates to real blows; we meet with such incidents also to-day in sham battles on the stage.

During these mysteries other scenes certainly took place as well, but were more restrained; of these however we have no record.

ACCOMPANIMENTS OF THE DANCE.

Rhythm is a common feature of dance, music and song, and for that reason the dance was linked up with music and song from the most remote times. Accompaniment of music and song had two advantages for the dance: the dancer listening to the rhythm did not deviate from it and thus his dance gained in accuracy. The coincidence of both rhythms enhanced the spectator's nejoyment, when emanating from the impressions of the eye and the ear.

Already in the picture emanating from prehistoric times found at El Amrah, the women dancers are accompanied by two men with clappers (fig. 1b).[41]) Judging by the pictures the most common accompaniment in the Old and Middle Kingdom consisted of clapping of hands, rhythmical shouts and songs (fig. 3—5, 8, 11, 12, 18, 26); neither in the latter times are clapping men and women

---

[40]) See *Erman-Ranke*, Ägypten und ägyptisches Leben im Altertum, pp. 318—319.

[41]) Compare this picture with fig. 37, where the man is beating time with two clappers.

lacking in pictures, even when the dancers are accompanied by instrumental music (35, 36, 40, 46, 54, 74, 75.) In fig. 26 the trainer is indicating time with shouts Ha, ha, ha, ha, i, i, i, i, which the painter wrote on the picture. This is probably the oldest preserved record of four-time measure. On the relief of the Cairo Museum (Musée égyptien I. tab. XXVI=Klebs, "Die Reliefs des alten Reiches", fig. 88, p. 108) we find illustrated a number of dancing women in postures similar to those in fig. 4, 5, 74 in front of whom two clapping women are standing and above this row there is another row of sitting musicians, a harp player and two pipers, who are given time by other men snapping their fingers. A similar scene is found in Lepsius' "Denkmäler", II, fig. 52, where besides a row of nine dancing men, depicted in similar positions as the women dancers in the preceding picture, we find two harp players, two pipers and opposite each of them a man beating time or singing. Whereas Klebs thinks that the artist intended to illustrate the synchronism of music and dance by the vicinity of these scenes, Montet considers this not to be the case. The vicinity of the musicians and the dancers is — according to him — to be attributed to the same aim of both scenes, viz. to entertain the master. The master was sometimes entertained by dancing only, without accompaniment of music, another time he listened to music only, but certainly often he joined both pastimes into a single one.

The accompaniment of dances by tambourines has been known from pictures of the Old Kingdom (fig. 51, 56, 58) but as tambourines are ancient instruments, they were used for accompaniment of dances much earlier. Since the New Kingdom, there accedes to the musical instruments accompanying the dance the lute (fig. 43–45) and the lyre (fig. 58), which were not known to the ancient Egyptians prior to this. By means of the lute the dancers often accompanied themselves (fig. 42, 50).[42])

---

[42]) See the chapter on the dance with musical instruments.

An unusual instrument for accompaniment of the dance was probably the great drum (fig. 60), or the boomerangs (fig. 61). In our pictures they are being used as an accompanying instrument to the dances of the Lybian and negro auxiliary troops.

THE DANCE WITH MUSICAL INSTRUMENTS.

In the earliest times the dance was accompanied by clapping of hands, snapping of fingers or knocking of clappers, later on by all musical instruments at hand. Still closer union of dancing and musical rhythm has been reached when the dancer accompanied himself, which meant of course a limitation of his movements.

If the dancers at harvest time or soldiers accompany themselves, beating two pieces of cane together (fig. 51, 57, 57, 58) they cannot reach the ground with their hands, nor can they deeply incline forward or backward. Should the dance lose thereby in wildness, it gains in exactness, refinement and grace.

Some other musical instruments require a quiet activity of the fingers and allow freedom of movement to the hands, so that the whole task is entrusted to the feet and the spine. In the New Kingdom the women dancers accompanied themselves most frequently on the lute (fig. 42, 50, 53, 62, 63), less customary was a person's own accompaniment on a double pipe (fig. 53, 54), probably because blowing the pipe hampers the respiration and very soon fatigues the dancer.

Very likely only during religious dances women danced with sistra (fig. 58). As a matter of fact the sistrum was not a musical, but magic instrument; its sound chasing evil spirits away.

Peculiar is the instrument in fig. 11 on the right[43]) with

---

[43]) In the original picture the dancers are arranged in two ranks; in the first rank there are four dancers in posture "a", then

which the dance has been performed; it consists of curved canes, which terminate in nicely made gazelles' heads; it is probably a rattle.[44]) Each of the women holds one in her left hand, the men in both hands.

three in posture "*b*" and three in posture "*c*"; in the second rank there were five women dancers in posture "*d*", the last of them, however, has been completely destroyed, all that has been left is only a small part of an uplifted hand; turned backward five dancers are dancing in posture "*e*", and facing them three clapping men are standing. The picture is rather damaged; not one single figure has been preserved completely; in our picture they are composed from all the preserved fragments.

[44]) *Curt Sachs* (D i e M u s i k i n s t r u m e n t e d e s a l t e n Ä g y p t e n s, p. 15) considers them to be clappers composed of two parts, similar to those held by the man on p. 36. *A. Wiedemann* (D a s a l t e Ä g y p t e n, p. 372), considers these instruments to be ritual instruments.

THE ELEMENTS OF THE ANCIENT EGYPTIAN DANCE.

The ancient Egyptian pictures and reliefs of women and men dancers allow us to form a clear idea what elements the ancient Egyptians availed themselves of in their dances.

I. MOVEMENTS OF THE LEGS.

In the fundamental ancient Egyptian step, when a movement forward was made, the leg on which the whole weight of the body rested was placed on the ground on the whole sole of the foot. The other leg was raised, stretched or slightly bent, the toes as a rule being inclined downward. Then the body inclined forward and the heel resting on the ground was raised up; the upraised leg was then lowered till it reached the ground, first with the toes and then with the whole sole of the foot.

This dancing step, somewhat unnatural and insufficiently elastic, is suitable for slow procedure; for a quick advance it is awkward. So far as we can observe on the pictures the heel of the foot on which the weight of the body rested was raised immediately when the other leg was lifted up, whereby the dancing step gained in elasticity.

In some pictures, especially in fig. 74, 76 the foot of the advancing leg forms a right or even a sharp angle to the shinbone, which does not give a good impression. Is it a lack of taste or is it a part of a compound dance-step? It is improbable that it may illustrate beating of time, because stamping with the bare heel is indistinct.

In fig. 38 a long step with the leg stretched out is illustrated, in fig. 11a, 12, 15, 23 the same step with the leg bent at the knee is depicted.

The opposing dancer in fig. 61 is drawn with a short completed thrust out, the individual women dancers in fig. 13 are starting a long advance, bringing the leg almost to split. The pairs in fig. 13 are also executing an advance; in the next moment one would expect them either to turn towards the spectator, the advance ending in a symmetrical posture of both dancers, or the advance might continue in the same direction in which it started. But that is less probable, because we should expect both dancers to raise the same leg at the same time.[45])

The only illustration of a rhythmical run will be found in fig. 56.

Skipping and jumps were elements used in dancing as frequently as steps.

In fig. 11b, c, we observe jumps almost finished; the front leg, almost stretched, rests on the ground already, the rear leg, bent at the knee, is still upraised and the centre of gravity of the whole body is shifting archwise above the front leg.

Jumps with legs together have been illustrated in fig. 36, 37, 60. Whereas the young men in fig. 36, 37 are jumping elastically, with bodies erect, the jump of the black

---

[45]) Judging by paragraphs 4 and 5 in the chapter dealing with the nature of the material p. 18 the original arrangement of the dancers is such:

the final arrangement:

is more probable than:

soldiers (on the left in fig. 60), who evidently are trying to imitate them, lacks in elegance. In fig. 31 *e, f*, two women are illustrated in various periods of the same jump with legs together, the woman "*e*" having got up curves the legs underneath, the woman "*f*" with legs drawn up to the body is sinking down; my doubt as to whether a jump forward or on the spot has been depicted, I have already expressed when dealing with the gymnastic dance.

Diminutive skipping on the spot or short jumps will be found by the reader in a number of instances, especially with regard to the dancers provided with musical instruments (fig. 42 and fol.). To distinguish here a step from a jump is of course difficult, because one cannot always trust the faithfulness of the reproductions, from which it has been copied. In this respect I draw attention to the final remark in the chapter dealing with the nature of the material.

In fig. 10 the woman standing on the left leg is thrusting the stretched right leg up to its height, inclining her body backward at the same time. It is not possible to decide whether this thrust may be an overture to a long step forward as has been the case with the individual dancers in fig. 13, or whether the dancers will turn from it to an erect position. The same thrust with the bent leg is executed by dancer "*e*" in fig. 11. The thrust of the leg by the right dancer of the left pair in fig. 33 probably means to illustrate a kick; the gesture of her retreating companion, avoiding the hit, points to this. Also crossing of the legs in fig. 26, 27 and 55 is a preparation for a thrust by legs carried forward into a position which will enable the dancer to get into rotation round his axis.[46])

---

[46]) The explanation that fig. 26 and 27 are representing a pirouette is more probable, than the explanation that the dancers in these pictures are executing a swing of the legs without turning. I have been led to this conclusion partly by comparison of fig. 55 with fig. 16—21, on which the dancers are executing a movement round their axis (in fig. 16—21 slowly, in fig. 55 in a swing), partly by the above quoted report of the young Syracusan regarding the

In a kneeling position we observe a girl in the dramatic dance fig. 28a, who represents the defeated enemy; then a girl dancing to the accompaniment of music in fig. 51, and finally in fig. 73 a praying girl. Most charming is the kneeling position of the girl in fig. 51, because the complete freedom of movement permitted her to choose such movements and postures which were aesthetically effective, whereas the kneeling girl in fig. 73 has been forced into an overextended kneeling position, having to bend low to the ground; the same applies to the girl in fig. 28, who is to collapse in a faint when the blow directed on her head will fall.

The postures of the dancing pair fig. 16–21 show that the dancers were performing turns-about of 180°, turning away and coming face to face again.

Somewhat enigmatic appears the performance of the woman dancer, illustrated in postures a–c fig. 31. The woman is standing on the left leg, keeping the right one bent at the knee and drawn close to the body. Probably the girl is not moving from the spot in a bound, because she would have been drawn at least once in the air, as is the case with the dancer "e", "f" in the same picture; judging by the inclination of the body and the position of the arms, it sooner appears that the dancer was only rhythmically swinging to and fro on one leg.

II. MOVEMENTS OF THE ARMS.

Whereas the legs bearing the weight of the body are rather restrained by this task in freedom of movement, the arms, if not otherwise occupied, are completely free, except where the movements or posture of the body require their cooperation.

---

dances at the banquet of the rich Egyptian, where pirouettes are being explicitly mentioned (see p. 32) beside somersaults illustrated in fig. 32. Attention is deserving fig. 26 and 27 as well as fig. 32 originating from the Middle Kingdom from the Beni Hassan tombs.

Where the women or men dancers accompany themselves on musical instruments, the movements of their arms are restrained by these instruments. Least in the way are the castagnettes, allusion to which has been made by the young Syracusan, who describes the banquet of the rich Egyptian of Memphis. Quite a number of them have been preserved.[47]) They are of small size, can be seized by the hand in such a way that on the picture one cannot perceive them. In my opinion they were used by the woman dancer in fig. 51 on the extreme left, and by the two women on the extreme right. This appears to give the only possible explanation why all three dancers indicated keep their hands clenched. Also the little girl in fig. 53 was probably holding castagnettes in her hands.

The double clappers also allowed sufficient movement for the dancer's hands, as we can observe in fig. 52 and 57. Both dancers in fig. 57 are drawn in a charming symmetrical posture. Their arms form the letter S. The right hand movement of the dancer on the left is gentler than that of her companion; this hand is probably tired.

Worse off were the dancers provided with small drums. The free hand had to strike the drum at given moments indicated by the music, whereby the liberty of their movements was considerably restricted. As with these women, the men dancers provided with canes (fig. 9) also lacked sufficient freedom of movement.

The women dancers accompanying themselves on double pipes fig. 42, 53, 54, or on the oboe fig. 52, were allowed very little freedom in their movements, being unable to remove their hands off the instruments, and still more restricted were the dancers holding lutes (fig. 42–53, 62, 63), here movements of their arms are out of the question.

In fig. 56 the dancers accompanying the god in a pro-

[47]) See *Curt Sachs*, D i e M u s i k i n s t r u m e n t e d e s a l t e n Ä g y p t e n s, Berlin 1921, pl. I, 9—11, p. 19—20, desription of the castagnettes all from the Berlin Museum.

cession lash the air with tree branches to chase evil spirits away. The movements of their arms are taken up not so much with the light branches as with the purpose; one has to admit that they knew how to give a natural charm to their movements.

Rather restricted in movements were pairs holding each other's hands fig. 16–21, executing symmetrical movements, each of them remaining at the same distance from the other almost all the time. They could bend or stretch their arms only moderately, raise or lower them only a little. The pairs in fig. 13 and 15 are holding both hands so that there remains little freedom for their arms and only by a moderate pull or pressure could they keep them in the required motion, and so correct the deviations which would disturb the final posture.

Some movements and postures of the body require certain movements of the arms, without which they would either be impossible, or by which at least they would be facilitated. In the span as in fig. 24, 25, 28b, 40, 41 on the right, the hands must give support to the body; to the dancers is left only the choice whether he or she wishes to keep the arms slightly curved in the elbows as in fig. 25, 40, 41, or whether he or she wants to bend them to a right angle as in fig. 25, or to stretch them to an outward arch as in fig. 24, 28b.

The dancers in fig. 10 keep the inclined part of their body in balance by outstretched arms. We see that slight shift of the centre of gravity to the right would be enough to make the dancer lose balance and collapse.

The dancers in fig. 35 have to support themselves with their hands placed on the ground, because without this support they would drop on their chests.

In fig. 26–27 movements are illustrated, which enable the dancer to turn round his axis by 360°. First of all he swings his arms in the opposite direction to which he intends to turn, in such a way that the body is driven to the desired movement by reaction. Then he stretches out his arm in the direction of its position to which he at first turns slowly, and at the end violently. He keeps also the second hand outstretched to get persistency in turning. By steadying and intensifying the movements of the arms he attains the about-turn exactly by 360°, not overreaching the completed circle.

The concurrent swinging of arms in fig. 31 induces the bodies of the dancers "a–c", standing on one leg, into swinging by way of reaction, these movements being inverse to those of the arms.

Even if we eliminate all the instances indicated, we cannot say that the dancers, both men and women, had complete freedom of movement of their arms.

If we compare all the ritual dances in fig. 3–5, 8, 23, 74–76 we find that the movements of their arms were restricted by rigid prescriptions, the most customary position of the arms in these dances – viz. the stretching out of the arms and their bending at the elbows so that the upturned palms almost meet above the head—occurs in fig. 4, 5, 8, 23, 74, which have been selected from a number of pictures identical with them in principle. The fact that this position of hands in dancing is a legacy of prehistoric times, as shown in fig. 1a, 1b, has been mentioned before.

Dancers with one arm extended and somewhat upward bent at the elbow may be found in fig. 3, 7, 76 and others not dealt with here. Since in fig. 75, 76 we find other movements of the dancer's arms also with the women lamenting at funerals (fig. 66–72) we come to the conclusion that these movements of arms had also been prescribed.

The observer who compares the dancers of the dwarf dances in fig. 59 with the two women dancers on the right in fig. 38, will be struck by the similar position of the fingers. The dancers of the dwarf dances in the tomb of Antefoker[48] have their right hand with their three outstretched and two clenched fingers in a similar position to the above

---

[48] *Davies*, The tomb of Antefoker, pl. XXII.

mentioned dancers in fig. 59, whereas the fingers of the left hand hanging freely along the body are loose. It is clear therefore that also here we meet with prescribed movements, and see into what details these prescriptions went. The co-incidence of the picture representing the dancing pair of men in the Paheri's tomb,[49]) with our picture 53, is also evidence thereof.

It is interesting to observe the degree to which the Egyptian dancers succeeded in illustrating an action, or a state of mind.

Fig. 61 convinces us that the war dance was executed in a very lively and natural manner; it gives us an impression that the dancers may abandon the dance at any time and start a real fight.

The woman in fig. 28a representing a king well illustrates with her right arm a swing with the club and her mate correctly lifts up the clenched fist to weaken the blow.

In fig. 28b the dancer illustrating the wind has no other option but to indicate the direction and the force of the wind by thrusting out her arms.

When an Egyptian wanted to address somebody, he stretched out his arm in a more or less bent way, so that the palm was on a level with his head. This position of hands as illustrated in fig. 3, 14, in the two middle women in fig. 33 and 34, in the jumping men in fig. 36, 37 and in the first two men in fig. 76, we find in the hieroglyphic determinatives accompanying words which mean "to speak", "to call" etc. There is no doubt that the two women dressed as men in fig. 14 are addressing the girl in the woman's garment facing them, whose quiet posture, freely hanging left arm, the right hand bent at the elbow and kept on the heart express rather an agreeable than an unpleasant feeling. This experience teaches us that the 8 women in fig. 33, 34 form four pairs of talking women, their postures seem to indicate comic scenes being performed. Enigmatic is the posture of the jumping man in fig. 36, 37.

[49]) See p. 38.

Eloquently has been expressed the bowing girl's humility in fig. 43, the respectful appeal of the middle girl, and the embarrassed attitude of the front girl in fig. 45, and the indecision expressed by the girl's movement of hands in fig. 50.

In the pictures representing funeral scenes, we meet again and again with expressions of grief, the most common among them being that indicated by the position of one or both arms extended forward and bent at the elbow with the palm placed upon the head (fig. 66–70, 72). We often find men and women with both arms either stretched forward or sideways and raised at elbows sometimes up to a right angle (fig. 66–69, 72), or lowered, or even with palms touching the ground (fig. 66, 67, 70, 71). We see two women with folded arms standing in the midst of the group in fig. 66 and the man in a sitting position in fig. 69. That these movements and postures were not always a natural expression but an adapted movement is evidenced in the simultaneous execution of this movement by several persons fig. 66 (the two middle women), 72, 76.

If the dancers — men or women — were completely free in their movements of arms, these were not to be indisciplined like those of the negro soldiers in fig. 60.

Quite often we find that movements of arms and hands correspond to the movements of legs and feet. So for instance in fig. 7 the woman dancer is standing on her right leg and her right arm is hanging freely along the body, the left leg and the left arm being raised in a moderately bent way. Similarly we find that the man "e" and the woman "d" in fig. 11, whose upraised arms and legs are markedly bent at the knees and elbows: the rattles provided with the antelopes' heads, which they hold in their hands, are no obstacle to their movements, on the contrary by appropriate position they add to the decorum of the dancers. The same predilection for conformity of movements of arms and legs may be observed among the solo dancers in fig. 13 and the jumping women in fig. 31.

Quite free appear to be the dancers' movements of arms in fig. 6 *a, b, c, in* fig. 11 and those of the women dancers fig. 12, 39, and in fig. 41 on the left.

When going once more through all those movements of arms in our pictures, we shall observe that the Egyptian women and men dancers evidently refrained from all movements requiring great tension of muscles, so as to avoid the impression of rigidity.

III. MOVEMENTS OF THE TRUNK.

The movements of the trunk may be classified from the technical point of view into forward inclines, reclines, sideways inclines, hip, belt, waist, and shoulder circuition. Dancers can combine these movements and execute them whilst keeping their spines stiff or accompany them by bending the spine forwards or backwards. Having regard to the manner of execution, one could distinguish movements performed at a normal speed from swings and retarded movements.

Instead of lengthy descriptions I shall confine myself to giving the readers a summary of the elements encountered in the trunk movements as gathered by analysis of the movements in our pictures:

Forward inclines: 11a, 17, 21, 28a, 29b, 33a, 33b, 34a, 34b, 34d, 39, 43, 44 45 middle, 47, 49 right, 51e, 53a, 57b, d, e, 60b, c, 61 left, 66b, c, d, h, 67, 68a, b, 70, 71, 73 below,
} alternative inclines and reclines 31a–c, 32,

Reclines: 10, 11b, c, e, 15b, 24, 25, 28b, 29a, c, 33d, 35, 40, 41, 54, 56a, b, 61 right,

Sideways inclines: 51c, d,
Hip circuition: 49 right,
Belt circuition: 15a, 45 left, 49 left,
Shoulder circuition: 16, 18, 19, 21, 33b, d, 34a, c, 43 standing girl, 45 right, 53a, 57a, 61b;

} 17, 20, 26, 27, 42 middle, 47, 50 middle, 51a, c, d, 56a, b, 57d, e, 61 right, } 51b, 53c, 57c, 60c,

Circuition with stiff spine: 11a, 25, 28a, 33b, 42middle, 43 (the standing girl), 45 both marginal figures, 50, 51a, 54, 57 a–c, 66d, 68a, 73 below; }

Circuition with spine bending forward: 31a, 33a, 39 in front, 43 bending, 45 middle, 57d, e, 66c, 67, 68b, 70, 71, } alternative: 32,

Circuition with spine bending backward: 10, 11e, 16–21, 24, 28b, 29a–c, 31b, 33d, 35, 39 rear, 40, 41, 47, 51a, d, e, 53a, c, 56a, b, 60b, c, 61, 66b, h; }

With a normal speed: 15a, 16, 18, 19, 21, 28a, 29b, 33d, 42 middle, 43, 45, 47, 51a, 53a, 60b, c;

With a swing: 10, 11a, b, c, e, 15b, 17, 20, 26, 27, 29a, c, 33a, b, 56a, b;

With a retarded movement: 24, 25, 28b, 31a, b, 40, 41, 66b, c, d, f, h, 67, 68, 70, 71, 73.

If we compare the movement of the trunk with the simultaneous movement of the limbs, we find that sometimes the movement of the body is dominating, another time its collaboration with the limbs is about equivalent, sometimes it plays a subordinate rôle, or the collaboration becomes altogether negative, as when the dancer by the rigidity of the body tries to evoke in the spectator an impression of bodily or mental lethargy.

A leading rôle by the trunk is played in pronounced reclines and spans fig. 10, 24, 25, 28e, 29a, 40, 41, in somersaults by pairs (fig. 32) and in bending performed in a recumbent position (fig. 35). The trunk is immovable in the ritual funeral dances (fig. 3, 4, 5, 7, 8, 23, 38, 59, 74, 75, 76).

COSTUMES OF THE ANCIENT EGYPTIAN
WOMEN AND MEN DANCERS.

The Egyptian dancers seldom wore the ordinary dress in dancing, viz. the white garment reaching up to the breast, supported by straps over the shoulders, and down to the ankles. We see the women in fig. 3, 4, 5, 12, 35, 36, 38, 75, dressed in this manner. On pictures originating from the Old Kingdom we observe women, dressed in this way, who are dancing the ritual funeral dance in fig. 8, and the dancer representing a woman dancing a lyrical dance in fig. 14; as for the Middle Kingdom, both acrobatic dancers in fig. 24 are dressed so and also the woman dancer in fig. 31d. With regard to the New Kingdom the middle dancer is so clad, representing a woman in fig. 50 and perhaps also the girl in fig. 52; and in the renaissance era the lamenting women in fig. 72 and the ritual dancers in fig. 75.

The reason why the women dancers wore so seldom this long garment for dancing is apparent. It obstructed their free movements, permitting merely short steps and short raising of the legs. That is why the women in the Old Kingdom put on men's skirts, consisting of a narrow strip of fabric hanging down from the belt, fastened round the hips and reaching above the knees, so that the body from the hips upwards remained uncovered. So clad are also the dancers in fig. 3, 4, 5, 11d, 12, 14, on the left. The dancers in fig. 7 and 10 in the middle of fig. 14 are dressed in men's aprons similar to a man's skirt, but cut round in the front, so that the legs are left free. In the front of the waist they wore a suspended panel hanging freely from the middle. In the Middle Kingdom the man's skirt as a woman dancer's costume is not known. The women dancers in fig. 25, 28 are dressed however in man's aprons without the scarf in front and we find these also on women of the New Kingdom (fig. 35, 38, 40, 41).

Quite nude are the little girls of the Old Kingdom in fig. 13; their mates in fig. 15 are provided with belts around their hips only.

In the Middle Kingdom the women dancers sometimes wore short women's garments reaching only above the knees, as can be observed in fig. 30–32; in the New Kingdom there is only one such case in fig. 34b.

Regardless whether the dancers of the New Kingdom danced naked, keeping a belt around their hips concealing however nothing, as in fig. 39, 42, 45, 48, 53a, or whether they were not completely nude as were the girls in fig. 53b, 57d, e and the dancers chasing evil spirits by their nudity in the religious procession in front of the god's shrine in the middle of fig. 58, these dancers adapted themselves to the reigning fashion, which was not so constant in the New Kingdom as in olden times.

In fig. 33 and 34 the dancers are dressed in narrow cloaks, opened in front, one side overlapping the other, in the lower part cut after the manner of the men's aprons but reaching down to the middle of the calves, the dancer in fig. 33d is in possession of a similar cloak, hanging from the left arm and leaving the right side of the chest uncovered.

The dancers in fig. 54 have short transparent garments, reaching up to the neck and down to the ankles; a similar garment, leaving the right breast uncovered is exhibited on the dancer playing on the lyre in fig. 50.

Women's ordinary dress in the New Kingdom consisted of a long broad cloak with either narrow or broad sleeves. Such transparent cloaks with narrow sleeves are exhibited on the dancers in fig. 43, 44, with wide sleeves in fig. 50 on the left, 51, 53c, 56, 57 except d, e, 58, 62. In fig. 51 the dancers wear belts under these cloaks, such as were worn by the nude dancers; in fig. 58 the dancers accompanying the shrine wear cloaks opened in front. Cloaks or sleeve less garments fitting tightly from top to waist, gathered around the hips and reaching down to the ankles, are worn by the dancers in fig. 49. A narrow sleeveless cloak or skirt with three flounces is worn by the woman dancer in King Amenhotep the IV's harem (fig. 63 in the centre). This foreign dress suggests that the dancer was not of Egyptian origin.

Quite unusual is the dancer's dress in fig. 47. She is garbed in a blouse with wide sleeves, the lower fringe of which can be distinctly seen from under the short gathered man's skirt.

The usual hairdress among the Egyptian women of the Old and Middle Kingdom consisted of long hair, evenly cut and smoothly combed down, divided into two thinner plaits hanging from the shoulders down to the chest and one broad plait, covering the upper part of the back. The women to whom nature was not quite generous in this respect supplemented the deficiency in hair by wigs, arranged in the same way. This arrangement of hair is illustrated best on the middle dancer fig. 50, on the clapping women fig. 54 and on the ritual dancers fig. 75. Apart from these, such hair arrangement is exhibited also in fig. 33, 34, on the clapping women fig. 35, 36, the clapping woman and the woman playing the oboe in fig. 52, on the dancers in fig. 56c and the mourning women in fig. 72. The dancer d in fig. 33 has her back stream of hair fastened with a ribbon.

The women dancers of the Old Kingdom wore their hair either shortly cut, or when it was worn long, then it was hidden under a tightly fitting cap, as in fig. 3, 4, 5, 7, 8, 11d, 12, 13, 15. In the New Kingdom hair so arranged is seen in fig. 35, 38, 43 in the middle, 46 in the middle, 51b–d and 52.

In fig. 10 and 14 almost all the dancers wear their hair

59

combed backwards, made up into one long pigtail cumbered at the end by a pretty large ball. This, however, may not be a hairdress at all but a tightly fitting cap, with a narrow long protrusion from the top, because such an arrangement is exhibited also by the men in fig. 6 and 13.

The hair combed backward and arranged into several pigtails provided with tassels at the end, is shown by the women dancers of the Middle Kingdom in fig. 24, 30–32, 43, 46 and of the New Kingdom in fig. 51a, e, 53b.

Peculiar is the hair arrangement of the middle dancer in fig. 28. The hair is wound round a firm frame, so that it is settled on the head in the same manner as the crown of the king of Upper Egypt, of which it reminds also by its shape.

Like the dress, so also the hair arrangements in the New Kingdom were more quickly influenced by changing fashions, whose obedient servants were also the Egyptian dancers.

Long loosely hanging hair is exhibited by the dancers in fig. 41, 45, 47, 58, shortly cut hair erroneously called bobbed hair (à la garconne) adorns the dancer's heads in fig. 41, 48, 49 and some of the dancers' heads in fig. 57.

Wigs of considerable size, as worn by the women of the New Kingdom, rest on the dancers' heads in fig. 39, 42, 53a, 56 and on some others in fig. 57. Remarkable hoods are found on the heads of the nude dancers in fig. 57d, e.

When other Egyptian women did not deprive themselves of ornaments, it is only natural that neither the women dancers would do without them. The most frequent ornaments were: Narrow or broader, brightly decorated collars, which the reader will find in fig. 3, 4, 5, 7, 10 of the Old Kingdom, fig. 30–32 of the Middle Kingdom, 38, 42, 45, 47, 49, 51, 58 of the New Kingdom and fig. 75 of the renaissance era.

Bracelets are found on the dancers' arms in fig. 5, 7, 10, 13, 24, 31, 32, 33, 34, 38, 39, 42, 43, 50, 51, 53a, b; on the feet in fig. 7, 10, 14, 24, 30, 31, 33, 34, 38.

Earrings are worn by dancers of the New Kingdom only as can be observed in fig. 39, 40, 42, 43, 46, 49–51.

Only in the Old Kingdom dancers wore ribbons round their chests, as the reader will find in fig. 4, 5, 11*d*, or wore ties on the neck fig. 7, 14.

Ribbons or garlands on the dancers' heads are found in the Old Kingdom only, see fig. 3; in the New Kingdom fig. 33, 34, 39, 42, 43, 46, 48, 51*a*, 52, 53*a*, 54, 57, and the mourning women in fig. 60, 67, 69, 70.

One woman of the Old Kingdom only in fig. 53c has a comb in her hair just as her mates playing on the lyre, harp, and the two clapping women in the sitting position.[50])

Flowers were often worn by the women in their hair, mostly favoured were lotuses, as witnessed by fig. 3, 7, 42, 43, 50, 53, 54, 66 on the right.

A very peculiar ornament — to our taste of course — was a cone made of semi-solid fat, saturated with scent, which was fastened on top of the head, so that the grease dissolving on the surface, trickled down the hair and dress, passing on to them its scent. The New Kingdom dancers in fig. 42–46, 53, 54 are provided with this ornament.

* *
*

The Egyptian men dancers wore as a rule the regular men's dress viz. a skirt (as regards the Old Kingdom, see fig. 11*a–c*, 12; as for the Middle Kingdom, fig. 23, 26 first on the right; the New Kingdom fig. 36 on the left, 55, 59, and the renaissance era, fig. 74–76), or an apron with round edges in the front; (with regard to the Old Kingdom see fig. 6, the Middle Kingdom, fig. 26, 29, 36, 47). If the first two men on the left in fig. 26 look as if they were dressed in bathing shorts, it is a deception caused by the painter illustrating incorrectly the front rounded part of the skirt. These skirts and aprons have been described before.

---

[50]) A comb can be distinguished from a ribbon in that way that it does not embrace the whole head ground as this does.

The dancers depicted in fig. 9 and 30 were provided with a belt and suspending panel. A belt with fringes in the front is worn by the pair dancers in fig. 16–21. Quite nude are the Old Kingdom boys in fig. 22 and the grown-up dancers in the ritual funeral dances of the renaissance period in fig. 76 on the left.

In fig. 36 and 37 appear men dressed in short women's garments; the jumping man in fig. 37 wears a still shorter woman's garment, cut out in the front in the manner of the man's apron, the probable reason being to accentuate the comical side of the scene presented.

Quite extraordinary seems to be the dress in fig. 27. The men wear probably quite a long and broad piece of material draped round the hips drawn in front under the belt and between the legs backward, the end of it being tucked in the belt at the back.

Men dancers had their hair always cut short. Sometimes they wore tightly fitting caps: so in the Old Kingdom fig. 11a–c, e, 12, 15⁻21; in the Middle Kingdom fig. 23, 26, 29, 30; in the New Kingdom fig. 30, 37, 53, in the renaissance era fig. 74, 76.

The dancers of the dwarf dances, which the reader will find in fig. 57, wore on their heads a crown woven of reeds or palm fibres into the shape of the white Upper Egyptian crown, quite similar to that of the hairdress of the women dancers in fig. 28a, b.

A cap with a long protrusion on the top, weighted with balls, familiar in the women dancers' headdress, is worn by a man in fig. 6.

Curls on the right temple are worn by the boys in fig. 22a–c.

In their desire for ornaments the Egyptian men dancers were, as it seems, much more modest than their mates. There are bracelets on the boys' feet in fig. 29, collars are worn by the men in fig. 6, 37; adorned with ties are the dancers in fig. 11a, b, c, 72, 75 and 76; head bound with ribbons exhibit only the dancers in fig. 23 and the man accompanying the dancing scene with clappers in fig. 36. These two men — our illustration showing only one — wear a chain round the neck, provided with a tassel at the back so as to keep the chain in the required position.

ANCIENT EGYPTIAN WOMEN AND MEN DANCERS.

About the ancient Egyptian women and men dancers we know so far very little.

A.

The narrative regarding the origin and birth of the first kings of the fifth Dynasty begins thus:[51])

One day Redzedet felt that labour pains were coming upon her. Then is Grace Ra, the Lord of Sakhebu told Eset, Nebthet, Meskhenet, Heket and Khnum: Go and help Redzedet in her delivery of the three children in her womb, who are predestined for the highest offices in this country. They will build temples for you, they will supply your offering tables, they will wreath your drink stands, and multiply your offering funds.

The goddesses departed, transformed themselves into vagrant musicians and dancers, and Khum went with them carrying a sack. When they arrived at the house of Rawoser, they found him standing enveloped in his cloak which he wore turned upside down. They started to clap and rattle with clappers and sistra, but he told them: "Look here, ladies, there is a woman in labour."

They told him: "Let us see her. We understand midwifery."

He replied: "Come in."

---

[51]) *Adolf Erman*, Die Märchen des Papyrus Westcar, Berlin, 1890, contains a heliographic reproduction of Mrs. Westcar's hieratic papyrus with a hieroglyphic transcription, first translation and commentary thereto.

A narrative of how Redzedet gave birth to the three future kings of the Upper and Lower Egypt now takes place and the text follows in this way:

Having liberated Redzedet of her three children, the goddesses came out and spoke thus: "Rejoice, Rawoser, three children have been born unto you."

He replied: "How can I reward you, ladies? Give this barley to your porter and take it to your granary."

Khnum put the sack of barley on his shoulder and they returned to where they came from.

Then Eset spoke to the gods: "How is it that we came to her and made no miracle for the children's sake, in order to report about it to their father who sent us?"

So they created divine crowns for the Lord — may he live, be fresh and enjoy health — and put them into the barley. Then they called for a storm and rain from the skies, came back and said: "May the barley be deposited here in a closed chamber, till we return on our way back northward!" The barley was deposited in a closed chamber.

The contents of this narrative are, of course, mythical. The Sun-god Ra, having begotten with Redzedet, wife of his high priest Rawoser, three sons, — the future kings — sent out four goddessess and the god Khnum to assist Redzedet in her labour and they completed their task satisfactorily. But in order to get to Rawoser's house unrecognised they turn into a group of vagrant dancers, and imitate them so naturally that Rawoser never suspected who came to his house disguised as dancers.

We gather then that vagrant dancers formed groups, each group of dancers had a permanent seat (take it to your granary) from which they set forth on their journeys. They were rewarded for their services with that which was given to them, and with it they returned home again.

Besides their art, they practised any other thing they knew to earn their daily bread. Their life did not, therefore, differ from the life of such artists as is described in Smetana's "Bartered Bride".

B.

Quite different was the fate of the harem women dancers of kings and princes. In fig. 62 we see a spacious hall and in fig. 63 two smaller rooms of the el-Amarna palace, belonging to king Ekhnaton (Amenhotep IV), in which the king's harem dancers practised dancing to the accompaniment of women musicians, playing on harps, lyres and guitars. In the right corner of the room there is a table with food on it and two stands with jugs of beer and wine. On the left, two doors lead to two chambers, in which supplies have been deposited. It is evident that the daily necessaries of these dancers were amply provided for. They lived quietly, without the worries which pursued their vagrant sisters.

C.

Among the hieratic papyri found in Kahun there is a fragment of an account-book from the Illahun temple of king Senwosret Kheperkare of the XII dynasty, who reigned from 1906–1887 B. C.[52]) On this fragment a note regarding the participation of men and women singers and dancers at the religious festivals has been recorded. We gather from it that in the Illahun temple there were five dancers of Asiatic origin, two dancers of negro origin, one Egyptian woman and four persons, the names of whom have been destroyed, so that we do not know either their origin or their sex.

Among the festivals during which they danced, the following are enumerated: The New Year, The Night Festival of Welcoming the Nile floods, Full and New Moon, the Festival connected with the five epagonal days,[53]) the God Sokar and Goddess Hathor Festival, Sand removal Festival, The Hitching of bulls to the harness for field work, and the Festival in honour of the King.

---

[52]) *F. Ll. Griffith,* H i e r a t i c P a p y r i f r o m K a h u n a n d G u r o b, London, 1898, pl. XXIV and XXV, pp. 59—62.

[53]) The Egyptian year had 12 months each of 30 days, after which 5 additional days followed, making together 365 days.

One can see that the Egyptians celebrated quite a number of festivals and that the staff of temple dancers could not complain of unemployment.

D.

When comparing the above indicated list of men and women dancers of the Illahum temple with the staff of women dancers accompanying the shrine of the god, carried in the religious procession illustrated on page 56, 58, we see that different kinds of persons are employed. In the first case we find an assembly composed of a majority of foreigners, which included one Egyptian woman only, whereas here a wide group of Egyptian women are seen and surely not of a low origin, if honoured to take part in a procession within close proximity to the god. In all probability they were trained amateurs of noble secular or priestly families.

E.

In the historical demotic novel of Vienna, dealing with king Petubastis[54]) the king sends out messages to various princes in Egyptian towns, in which he summons them to participate actively at the funeral ceremonies for the deceased King (see below, next paragraph) Yenharrou. The prince of the Eastern country, Peklul, having received the king's message, admonishes his son, saying:

"My son, Pemu, go and see to.....the troops of the eastern country, have them prepared with their girdles and myrrh, with the temple officials, masters of ceremony and dancers, who frequent the embalming rooms. Let them sail by boat to Per–Osiris, let them convey (the deceased body) of Osiris, the King Jenharrou to the anointing room, have him embalmed and buried and arrange a beautiful, grand

---

[54]) The demotic text has been published by *Jacob Krall*, D e-m o t i s c h e L e s e s t ü c k e I, Wien, 1897, pl. XVII; II, Wien, 1903, pl. X.—XII.; the last published edition: *Wilhelm Spiegel-berg*, D e r S a g e n k r e i s d e s K ö n i g s P e t u b a s t i s, Leipzig, 1910, pp. 46—75.

funeral for him such as is being prepared for Hapi (Great Apis) and Merwer (Greek Mnevis), the King of the gods."

We gather then that the Egyptian towns kept also special ritual dancers.

NOTE ON THE HISTORICAL DEVELOPMENT OF THE ANCIENT EGYPTIAN ART OF DANCING.

All our pictures of the ancient Egyptian dances have been arranged in chronological order:

Fig. 1 and 2 originate from prehistoric times, which end about the second half of the fourth millenium B. C.

Fig. 3–22 originate from the old Kingdom (III–VI Dynasty) the end of which is put at the beginning of the 23rd century B. C.

Fig. 23–32 are Middle Kingdom products of the XII Dynasty, whose kings reigned in Egypt from 2000 to 1788 B. C.

Fig. 33–71, 73 belong to the era of the greatest prosperity of Egypt, to the New Kingdom (XVIII–XX Dynasty) 1580–1090 B. C.

Fig. 72, 74–76 originate from the Renaissance era (XXVI Dynasty) 663–525 B. C.

I do not consider this material sufficient for formation of an opinion on the historical development of the ancient Egyptian art of dancing.

The judgment is correct that the dances, which we find on these pictures from a certain epoch, were really performed at that time, because these pictures of dancing scenes have been taken out of a great number of other pictures, representing realistically the life of the Egyptians at that time. We find there artists, artisans, farmers, building workers, hunters of game, fish and birds, women doing housework, scribes working in offices, gentry at banquets, audiences at the king's court, military drill etc. Since all these scenes endeavour to depict reality, we may rightly judge that also the dancing scenes represent realistic postures and movements of the contemporary women and men dancers.

A logical error has been committed by Luise Klebs and all others, who think that in a certain period some dances did not occur, because they have not been documented by contemporary pictures, forgetting that such pictures might have existed but have not been preserved up to our times, or which still may be found hidden under layers of sand in the so far undiscovered tombs, or finally that the Egyptian artists did not draw them for various reasons. A warning against this error of logic we find in the description of the feast in the house of the Egyptian of Memphis, given by the Syracusan visitor to Egypt. According to one part of this description, alluded to on page 32, we see that in the fourth century B. C. the same acrobatic dances were in vogue, which we know from the pictures originating in the XX century B. C. Their existence in this late period would have been utterly unknown to us, were it not for this accidentally preserved Greek description. Who can affirm that the Egyptians of the Middle Kingdom did not know also the lyrical dances, which have been described by the same Syracusan in another part of his description, referred to on page 24.

I conclude, therefore, that one may with certainty sketch only the development of such cultural elements where considerable materials from all times have been preserved, such as the Egyptian writing, language, and costumes, but not such elements of which only an insufficient material, as for instance dances, *belles-lettres,* mysteries and others have been preserved.

NOTE ON THE EGYPTIAN DANCES,
AS PERFORMED BY MODERN WOMEN DANCERS.

If we go once more through the pictures representing ancient Egyptian dances, and if we read through the chapters on the elements of movements of the dances, we have to confess that there is nothing that would not be known to the contemporary art of dancing.

Apart from pictures 33, 34, 72, 75, nowhere do we find angular movements in bending of limbs, witnessing to jerky movements, with which we are regaled by modern women dancers, passing off their art as Egyptian. In fig. 33 and 34 the angular, but not jerky movements are to evoke an impression of grotesqueness; in fig. 72 the unpleasant impression of rigidity has not been called forth by the posture as such, but by the fact that the movement is being performed by six persons, lined up in two ranks, and almost covered up. Picture 75 originated really from the renaissance era, when the Egyptian culture was in decadence. The Egyptians tried to wade out of it by reviving old cultural elements. The Egyptian plastic artists however did not create, but only copied old models; so for instance our fig. 75, 76 come from the tomb of Aba, who had had copied upon its walls pictures of another Aba of the Old Kingdom, who lived 18 centuries before him. The awkwardness of the postures are therefore to be attributed more to the mercenary copyist of the 7th century B. C. than to the artistic creator of the 25th century B. C.[55])

[55]) Reproduction of the reliefs from the tomb of Aba of the Old

A question arises therefore, from where did the present day dancers acquire those tasteless movements and postures which they pass off as Egyptian? In vain I searched for them in the ancient Orient, in Greece and Rome, till I found them among the Etruscans. In fig. 77, 78 I show a specimen of four pictures of men and women dancers from the Etruscan tombs, drawn from fig. 207 and 214 of Fritz Weege's work, "Der Tanz in der Antike", Halle a. d. Saale 1926, where the reader will find some 40 more of them, different in detail but equally characteristic.

Kingdom has been published by *Davies* in his book D e i r e l G e b-r â w i I; it is clear, that the first three women in fig. 75 are reproductions of women bearing offerings on their head; hence their unusual position of the hands.

SUPPLEMENT

1. The chapter on dancing with musical instruments is to be supplemented by a sketch originating from the XVIII Dynasty, which has been published in 1934 by Bernard Bruyère in his treatise Fouilles de Deir el Medineh, 1931—1932, page 71.

The artist has illustrated women dancers accompanying themselves by clackers. The manner in which the drawing has been executed, is rather unusual with the Egyptians. The painter, who did not keep to the prescriptions here, which elsewhere he was obliged to observe, has evaded the rigidity apparent from other pictures drawn in the traditional way and so has attained very effective vivacity. From the postures represented we may infer a purely movemental dance, reminding us of Spanish dances with castagnettes.

II. For sake of completeness a partly preserved picture from the ruins of the Temple of Bubastis has also been added. This has been published in 1892 by Edouard Naville in his work: Festival Hall of Osorkon II in the great Temple of Bubastis, pl. XV. No 5.

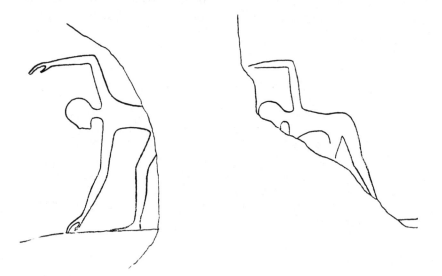

This is a reproduction of fragments of a picture, illustrating a religious festival, which in Egypt was always accompanied by dancing. L. Klebs has published this picture in her book: Die Reliefs und Malereien des neuen Reiches p. 225, fig. 140. and considers the postures to represent a phase of a star. I disagree with this view, because to my idea the Egyptians, who were used to depict the most characteristic position of the dancer, would have drawn either one or both legs in the air.

BIBLIOGRAPHY.

Marie Luise Becker, D e r T a n z, Leipzig, 1901.
Miloslav Beránek, N o v ý n á z o r o p r o s t o r u v u m ě n í s t a r é -
h o E g y p t a, Veraikon, roč. VI, 1919–1920.
Gustave le Bon, L e s p r e m i è r e s c i v i l i s a t i o n s, Paris.
N. Bouriant, T o m b e a u d e H a r m h a b i, Mémoires publiés par
les membres de la Mission archéologique française du Caire, V,
3–4, Paris, 1894.
Jean Capart, L e s d é b u t s d e l'a r t e n É g y p t e, Bruxelles, 1904.
N. de G. Davies, T h e m a s t a b a o f P t a h h e t e p a n d A k h e t -
h e t e p a t S a q q a r e h, Publications of the Archeological Sur-
vey of Egypt VIII, IX, 1897–1899.
— T h e r o c k t o m b s o f S h e i k h S a ï d, Publications of the
Archaeological Survey of Egypt X, 1899–1900.
— T h e r o c k t o m b s o f D e i r e l G e b r â v i, Publications of
the Archaeological Survey of Egypt XI, XII, 1900–1902.
— T h e t o m b o f A n t e f o k e r, v i z i e r o f S e s o s t r i s I
a n d o f h i s w i f e S e n e t, The Theban tombs series II, Lon-
don, 1920.
— T h e r o c k t o m b s o f E l A m a r n a III, Publications of the
Archaeological Survey of Egypt, XV, 1905.
Adolf Erman, D e r B r i e f d e s K ö n i g s N e f r - k è̕ ̕ '-r e', Zeitschrift
für die aegyptische Sprache und Altertumskunde XXXI, 1893.
— A e g y p t e n u n d a e g y p t i s c h e s L e b e n i m A l t e r-
t u m, n e u b e a r b e i t e t v o n *Hermann Ranke,* Tübingen, 1923.
Alan H. Gardiner, D i e E r z ä h l u n g d e s S i n u h e u n d d i e H i r-
t e n g e s c h i c h t e, Hieratische Papyrus aus den königlichen
Museen zu Berlin V, Leipzig, 1909.
F. Ll. Griffith, H i e r a t i c p a p y r i f r o m K a h u n a n d G u r o b,
London, 1898.
F. Ll. Griffith and *Percy E. Newberry,* El. Bersheh, Publication of
the Archaeological Survey of Egypt III, IV, 1892–1894.
A. E. J. Holwerda, D i e D e n k m ä l e r d e s a l t e n R e i c h s, Be-
schreibung der aegyptischen Sammlung des niederländischen
Reichsmuseum der Altertümer in Leiden I, Leiden, 1905.

Luise Klebs, Die Reliefs des alten Reiches.
— Die Reliefs und Malereien des mittleren Reiches, Abhandlungen der Heidelberger Akademie der Wissenschaften, Phil.-hist. Klasse, 3., 6. Abhandlung, Heidelberg 1915, 1922.

Jakob Krall, Demotische Lesestücke I, Wien, 1897.

Richard Lepsius, Denkmäler aus Aegypten und Aethiopien, Berlin, 1849–1858.

František Lexa, Beletristická literatura staroegyptská I, Knihy východní IX, Kladno, 1923.
— Obecné mravní nauky staroegyptské III, Nauka Aniova a Amenemopetova, Facultas philosophica universitatis Carolinae Pragensis, Sbírka pojednání a rozprav XIII, Praha, 1929.

Auguste Mariette-bey, Dendérah, Paris, 1870–1875.

Pierre Montet, Scènes de la vie privée dans les tombeaux égyptiens de l'ancien empire, Publications de la faculté des lettres de l'université de Strasbourg XIV, Strasbourg, 1925.

Alexandre Moret, Mystères égyptiens, Paris, 1923.

Edouard Naville, The temple of Deir e Bahari IV, Publications of the Egypt Exploration Fund, XIX, 1901.

Percy E. Newberry, Beni Hasan I, II, Publications of the Archaeological Survey of Egypt I, II, 1890–1892.

W. M. Flinders Petrie, Deshâsheh, Publications of Egypt Exploration Fund, XV, 1895–1896.

W. M. Flinders Petrie and *J. H. Walker,* Qurneh, Publications of the Egyptian Research Account IX, 1909.

J. E. Quibell, The Ramesseum, Egyptian research account II, 1896.
— The tomb of Yuaa and Thuiu, Catalogue général des antiquités égyptiennes du Musée du Caire. XLIII, 1908.

Rituale für den Kultus des Amon und für den Kultus der Mut, Hieratische Papyrus aus den königlichen Museen zu Berlin I, Leipzig, 1901.

Curt Sachs, Die Musikinstrumente des alten Aegyptens, Staatliche Museen zu Berlin, Mitteilungen aus der aegyptischen Sammlung III, Berlin, 1921.

Heinrich Schäfer, Von aegyptischer Kunst, Leipzig, 1919.

V. Scheil, Le tombeau de graveurs.
— Le tombeau de Rat'eserkasenb.
— Le tombeau d'Aba.
Mémoires publiés par les membres de la Mission archéologique française du Caire V, 3–4, Paris, 1894.

Select Papyri in the hieratic character from the collections of the British Museum, London, 1842–1860.

Kurt Sethe, Urkunden des alten Reiches.
– Urkunden der 18. Dynastie I. Leipzig, 1903, 1906.
– Urkunden des aegyptischen Altertums I, IV, Leipzig, 1903, 1906.
– Die altägyptischen Pyramidentexte, Leipzig, 1909–1910.

Wilhelm Spiegelberg, Der Sagenkreis des Königs Petubastis, Leipzig, 1910.

I. J. Tylor, The tomb of Sebeknekht, Wall Drawings and Monuments of El Kab, London, 1896.

I. J. Tylor and *F. Ll. Griffith*, The tomb of Paheri at El Kab, Publications of Egypt Exploration Fund XI London, 1894.

Ph. Virey, Le tombeau de Rekhmara préfet de Thèbes de la XVIIIᵉ dynastie, Mémoires publiés par les membres de la Mission archéologique française du Caire V, 1, Paris 1889.

Fritz Weege, Der Tanz in der Antike, Haale/Saale, 1926.

Arthur Weigall, Ancient Egyptian works of art, London, 1924.

A. Wiedemann, Das alte Aegypten, Heidelberg, 1920.

J. Gardner Wilkinson, Manners and customs of the ancient Egytians, including their private life, governement, laws, arts, manufactures, religion, agriculture and early history, derived from a comparison of the paintings, sculptures and monuments still existing with the accounts of ancient authors, London, 1837.
– A popular account of the ancient Egyptians, new edition, London, 1874.
– The Manners and customs of the ancient Egyptians, a new edition revised and corrected by *Samuel Birch*, London, 1878.

Walter Wreszinski, Atlas zur altaegyptischen Kulturgeschichte I, Leipzig, 1923.

II. SKETCHES

LIST OF PICTURES AND THEIR ORIGIN.

Fig. 1, 2: *Capart*, L e s d é b u t s d e l'a r t, page 116, fig. 83.

Fig. 3: *Schäfer*, V o n ä g y p t i s c h e r K u n s t II, pl. 23, fig. 1. = *Lepsius*, D e n k m ä l e r II, pl. 36.

Fig. 4: *Montet*, L e s s c è n e s d e l a v i e p r i v é e, pl. XXIV 2.

Fig. 5: *Becker*, D e r T a n z, page 7, fig. 2. = *Lepsius*, D e n k m ä l e r II, pl. 101 b (there are four women dancers and two clapping women).

Fig. 6: *Davies*, D e i r e l G e b r â w i I, pl. X (there are three more pairs of women dancers in the same attitude).

Fig. 7: *Davies*, D e i r e l G e b r â w i II, pl. XVII (behind the woman dancer with flowers on her head, there is another dancer now completely destroyed and still another partly destroyed; behind them, however, there is a partly preserved figure of a man in a sitting attitude playing on harp).

Fig. 8: *Klebs*, R e l i e f s d e s a. R., page 44, fig. 30. = *Lepsius*, D e n k m ä l e r II, pl. 35 (Four women in the same attitude are dancing in front of a dining table, behind the table facing them are standing three women, clapping their hands).

Fig. 9: *Lepsius*, D e n k m ä l e r III, pl. 56 (There were originally five dancing men).

Fig. 10: *Klebs*, D i e R e l i e f s d e s a. R., page 111, fig. 89. = *Capart*, U n e r u e d e s t o m b e a u x, pl. LXIX (the women dancers are at least four; *facing* them are several women clapping (?) their hands dressed in the customary women's garmens; the first one is encouraging them with hands raised up; see *Weege*, D e r T a n z i n d e r A n t i k e, page 23, fig. 21.

Fig. 11: *Petrie*, D e s h a s h e h, pl. XII (figures "a—e" are selected out of two lines of men and women dancers greatly damaged; in the first line there were four men in the attitude "a", three men in the attitude "b", three men in the attitude "c"; in the rear line there were five women in the position "d", four men in the position "e" and three men clapping).

Fig. 12: *Davies,* S h e i k h S a ï d, pl. IV (to the left there is one more woman clapping, to the right three more women dancers in an attitude identical with that of of the first woman).

Fig. 13: *Davies,* D e i r e l G e b r â w i II, pl. VII.

Fig. 14: *Davies,* D e i r e l G e b r â w i II, pl. XX.

Fig. 15: *Davies,* D e i r e l G e b r â v i II, pl. VII (on the left from the pair "*a*" there are standing 5 clapping men, dressed in men's skirts; between pair "*a*" and "*b*" are standing three clapping men without skirts facing pair "*b*").

Fig. 16—21: *Wilkinson,* M a n n e r s a n d C u s t o m s II, page 337, fig. 240.

Fig. 22: *Davies,* P t a h h e t e p I, pl. XXI.

Fig. 23: *Griffith,* E l B e r s h e h II, pl. XIV (behind the dancer on the left there follow some more dancers in the same attitude, three of them only being partly preserved).

Fig. 24: *Newberry,* B e n i H a s s a n II, pl. IV (also pl. XIII).

Fig. 25: Z e i t s c h r i f t f ü r d i e a e g. S p r a c h e XXXVII, 1899, page 77.

Fig. 26: *Newberry,* B e n i H a s s a n II, pl. XIII (also pl. XVII).

Fig. 27: *Newberry,* B e n i H a s s a n II, pl. VII (also pl. XVII) (facing the dancers are standing four clapping men).

Fig. 28: *Newberry,* B e n i H a s s a n I, pl. XXIX.

Fig. 29: *Newberry,* B e n i H a s s a n I, pl. XIII (on the left from this group a man is standing facing it with hands raised above his head).

Fig. 30: *Newberry,* B e n i H a s s a n II, pl. IV.

Fig. 31: *Newberry,* B e n i H a s s a n II, pl. IV (also pl. XIII).

Fig. 32: *Newberry,* B e n i H a s s a n II, pl. XIII (also pl. IV).

Fig. 33, 34: *Petrie,* Q u r n e h, frontispiece.

Fig. 35: *Davies,* A n t e f o k e r, pl. XV.

Fig. 36: *Wilkinson,* M a n n e r s a n d c u s t o m s II, page 257, fig. 198 (behind the man with clackers is standing his mate in the same attitude; see *Wreszinski,* A t l a s, pl. 267 B).

Fig. 37: *Davies,* A n t e f o k e r, pl. XV.

Fig. 38: *Davies,* A n t e f o k e r, pl. XXIII.

Fig. 39: *Wilkinson,* M a n n e r s a n d c u s t o m s II, page 390, fig. 279 (on the left from the dancers is a table with jug of wine, on the left four women are sitting on the ground, one of whom is blowing a double pipe, the others applauding the dancer).

Fig. 40: *Weigall,* A n c i e n t E g y p t i a n W o r k s o f A r t, page 152.

Fig. 41: *Sachs,* D i e M u s i k i n s t r u m e n t e, page 38, fig. 35 (the original exhibits two more identical lines above our illustration).

Fig. 42: *Weigall,* A n c i e n t E g y p t i a n W o r k s o f A r t, page 152.

Fig. 43: same author, fig. 44: *Bouriant*, T o m b e a u d e H a r e m-
h a b i, pl. II.

Fig. 44: = fig. 43: *Wilkinson*, M a n n e r s a n d c u s t o m s II, pl.
XII.

Fig. 45: *le Bon*, L e s p r e m i è r e s c i v i l i s a t i o n s, page 77, fig. 45.

Fig. 46: *Wilkinson*, M a n n e r s a n d c u s t o m s II, page 236,
fig. 188.

Fig. 47: *Wilkinson*, M a n n e r s a n d c u s t o m s II, page 301,
fig. 222.

Fig. 48: *le Bon*, L e s p r e m i è r e s c i v i l i s a t i o n s, page 77,
fig. 46.

Fig. 49: *Bouriant*, T o m b e a u d e H a r e m h a b i, pl. I (on the left
a harp player is standing and behind her a clapping girl is
sitting).

Fig. 50: *Wreszinski*, A t l a s, pl. 259.

Fig. 51: *Wilkinson*, M a n n e r s a n d c u s t o m s II, page 329,
fig. 235.

Fig. 52: *Sachs*, D i e M u s i k i n s t r u m e n t e d e s a. A e g., page 13,
fig. 4.

Fig. 53: *Scheil*, T o m b e a u d e R a t e s e r k a s e n b, pl. II.

Fig. 54: *Wilkinson*, M a n n e r s a n d c u s t o m s II, page 312,
fig. 228.

Fig. 55: *Virey*, L e t o m b e a u d e R e k h m a r a, pl. XXI.

Fig. 56: *Wilkinson*, M a n n e r s a n d c u s t o m s II, page 240,
fig. 195.

Fig. 57: *Becker*, D e r T a n z, page 11, fig. 4.

Fig. 58: *Wiedemann*, D a s a l t e A e g y p t e n, fig. 26.

Fig. 59: *Wilkinson*, A p o p u l a r a c c o u n t I, page 102, fig. 110.

Fig. 60: *Wilkinson*, M a n n e r s a n d c u s t o m s II, page 264,
fig. 201.

Fig. 61: *Naville*, D e ï r e l B a h a r i IV, pl. 90.

Fig. 62: *Davies*, E l A m a r n a III, pl. XXXIII.

Fig. 63: *Erman-Ranke*, A e g y p t e n, page 80, fig. 27.

Fig. 64, 65: *Quibell*, T o m b o f Y u a a, pl. XXXIX, XLI.

Fig. 66: *Wilkinson*, M a n n e r s a n d c u s t o m s I, page 256, fig. 7.

Fig. 67—69: *Scheil*, T o m b e a u d e g r a v e u r s, pl. VIII, VII,
VI (excerption of funeral scenes).

Fig. 70: *le Bon*, L e s p r e m i è r e s c i v i l i s a t i o n s, page 207,
fig. 101 (excerption of funeral scene).

Fig. 71: *Wreszinski*, A t l a s, pl. 421 (excerpt from a funeral scene).

Fig. 72: *Scheil*, T o m b e a u d'A b a, pl. IX.

Fig. 73: *Weigall*, A n c i e n t E g y p t i a n w o r k s o f a r t, page
300, 301.

Fig. 74: *Wilkinson*, M a n n e r s   a n d   c u s t o m s   II, page 336, fig. 238 (the man is taken out of a row of eight dancers, in the head of which two leading dancers are marching, the lines being closed by two clapping women; see *Scheil*, T o m b e a u   d'A b a, pl. II, the upper line).

Fig. 75, 76: *Scheil*, T o m b e a u   d'A b a, pl. II, lower row.

Fig. 77, 78: *Weege*, D e r   T a n z   i n   d e r   A n t i k e, page 145, fig. 214, page 142, fig. 207.

Figs. 1–2

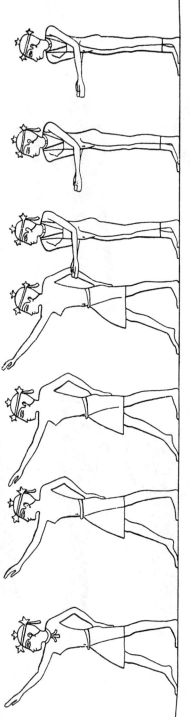

Fig. 3

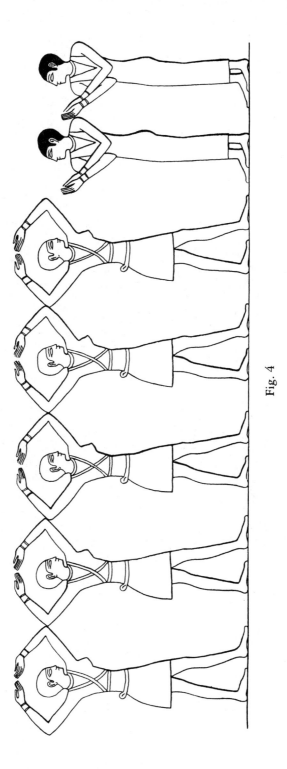

Fig. 4

87

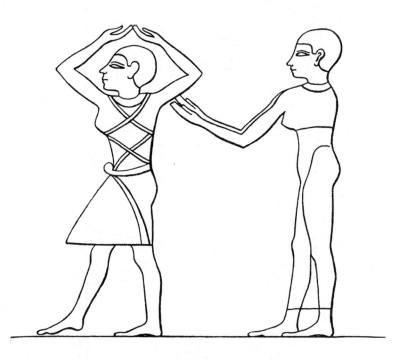

Fig. 5

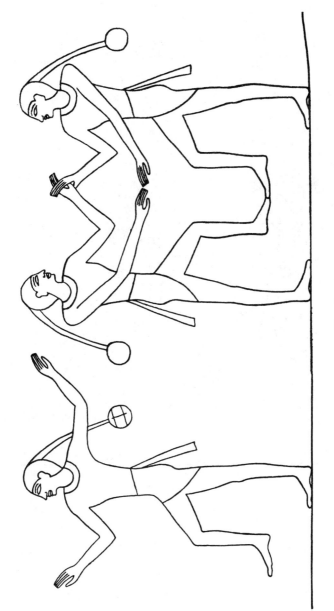

Fig. 6

89

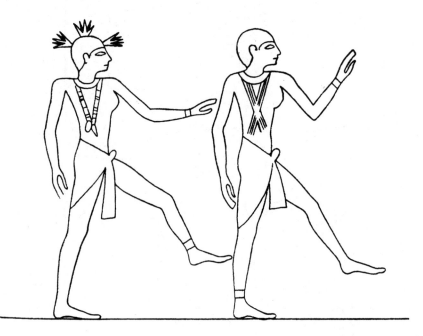

Fig. 7

Fig. 8

Fig. 9

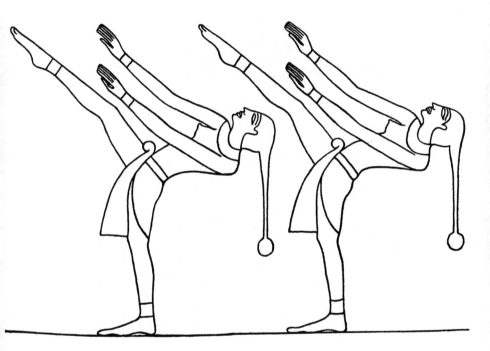

Fig. 10

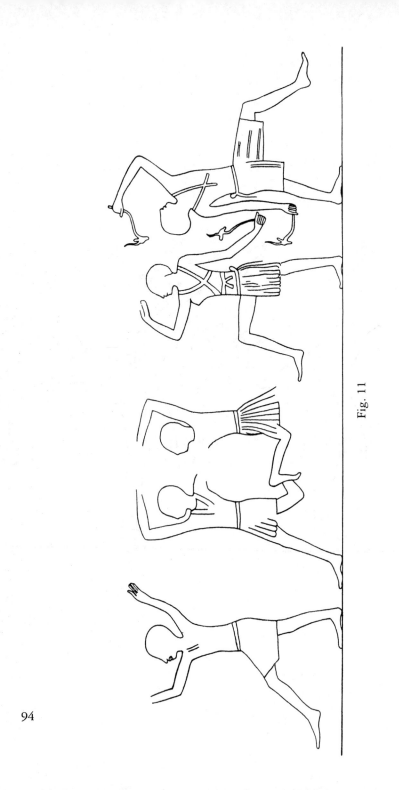

Fig. 11

94

Fig. 12

Fig. 13

Fig. 14

98

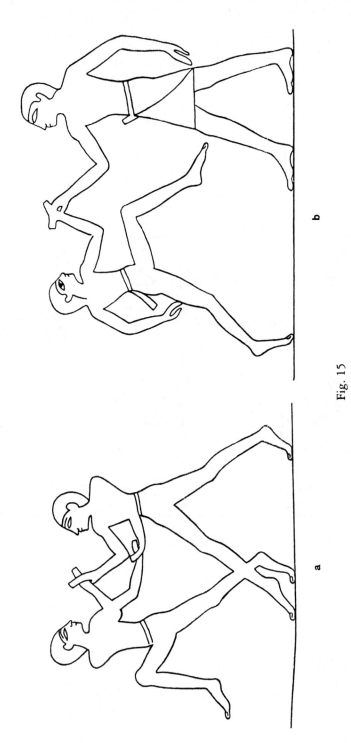

Fig. 15

a

b

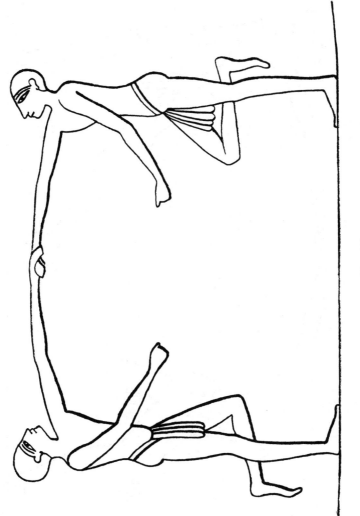

Fig. 16

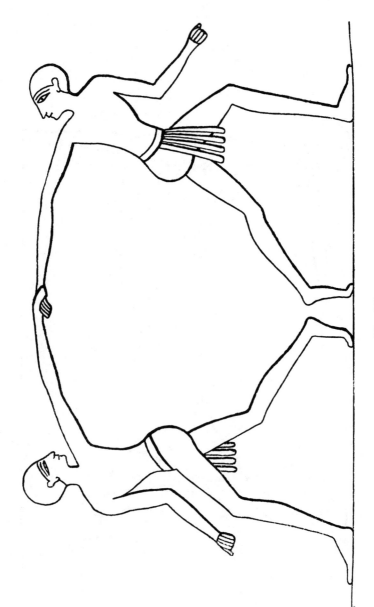

Fig. 17

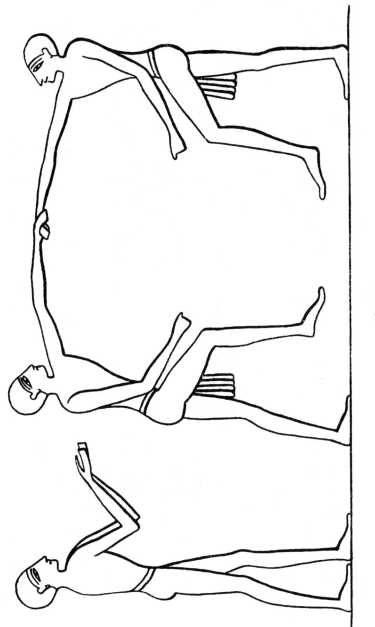

7   Fig. 18

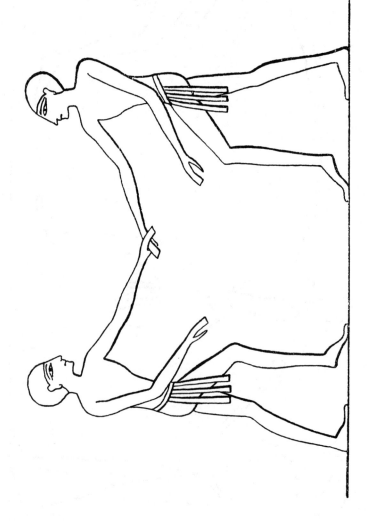

Fig. 19

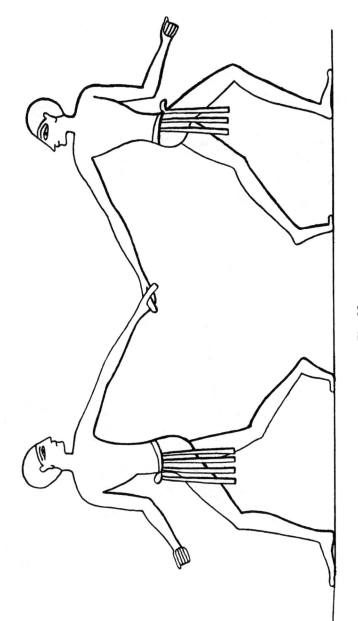

Fig. 20

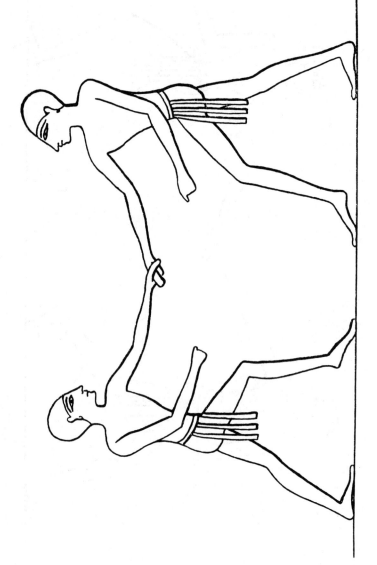

Fig. 21

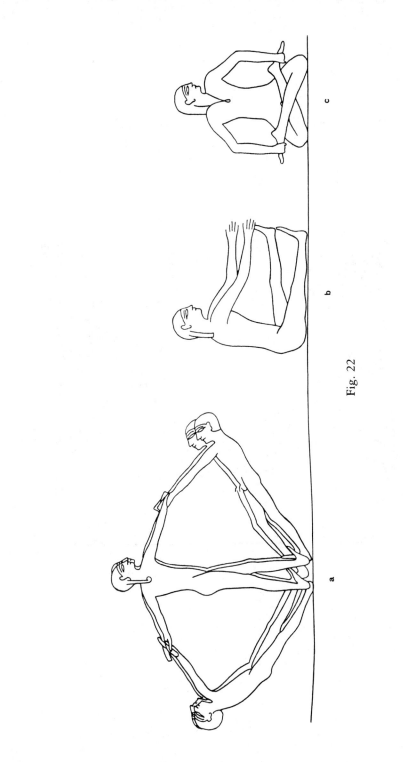

Fig. 22

105

Fig. 23

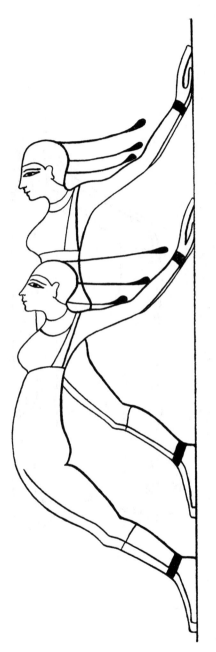

Fig. 24

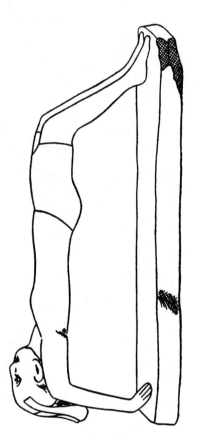

Fig. 25

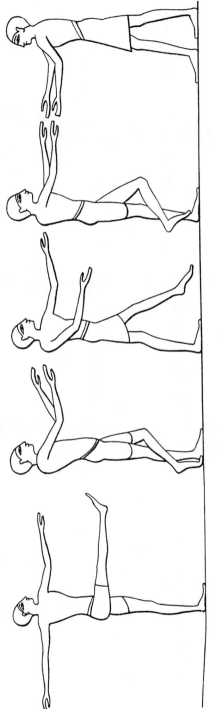

Fig. 26

Fig. 27

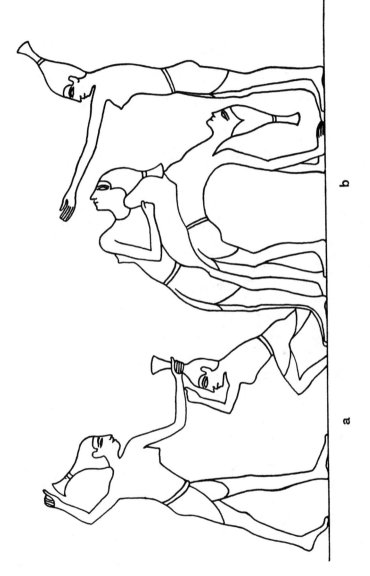

Fig. 28

a   b

112

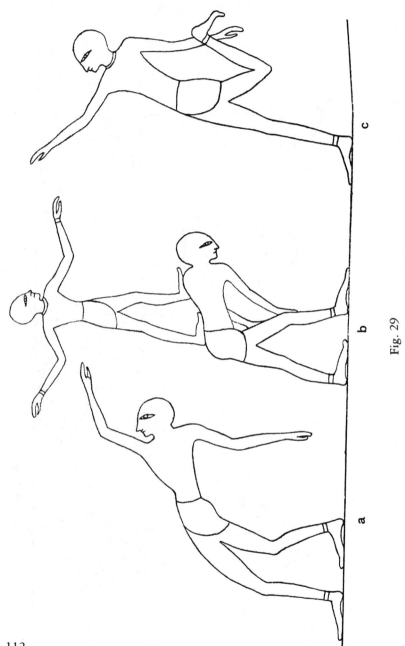

a

b

c

Fig. 29

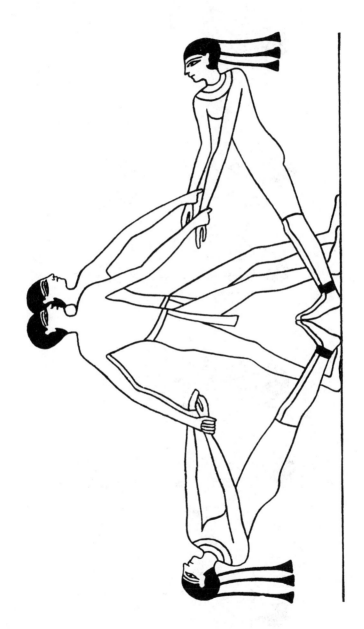

Fig. 30

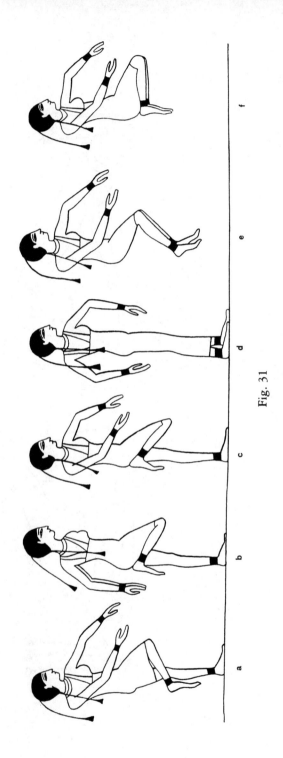

Fig. 31

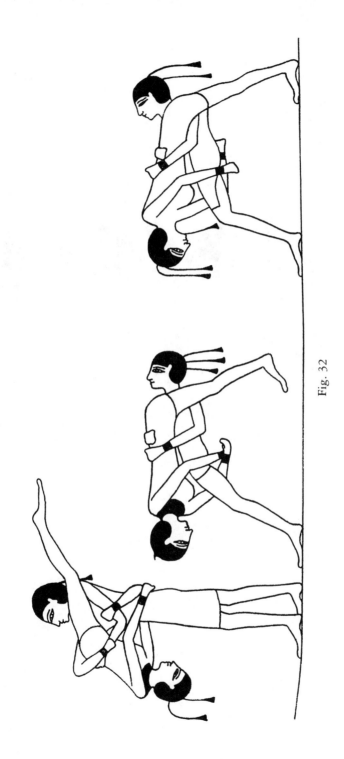

Fig. 32

a   b   c   d

Figs. 33–34

Fig. 35

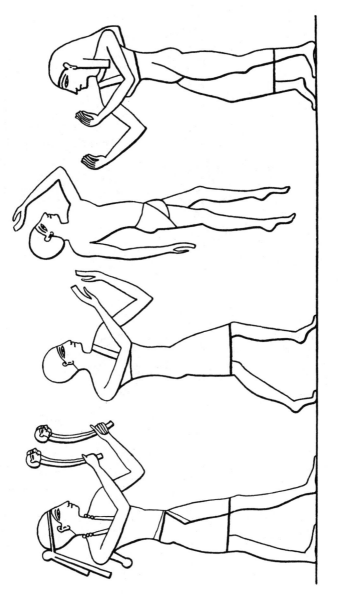

Fig. 36

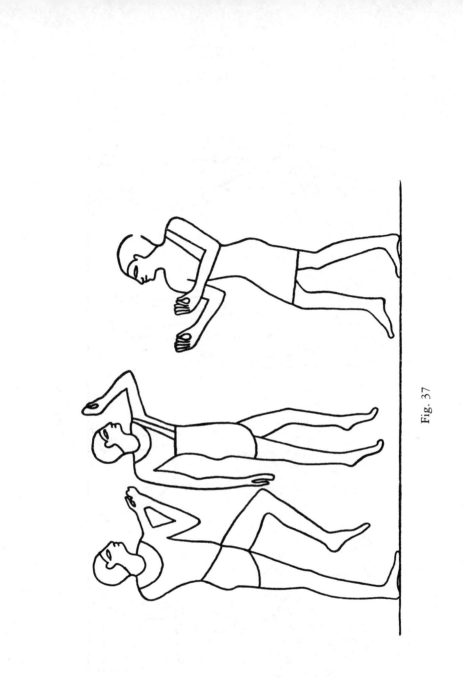

Fig. 37

Fig. 38

Fig. 39

Fig. 40

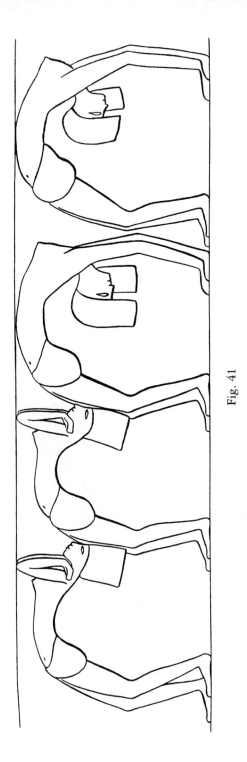

Fig. 41

Fig. 42

Fig. 43

Fig. 44

Fig. 45

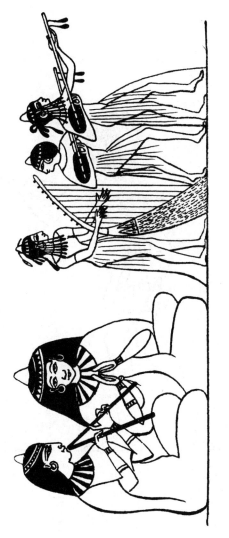

Fig. 46

Fig. 47

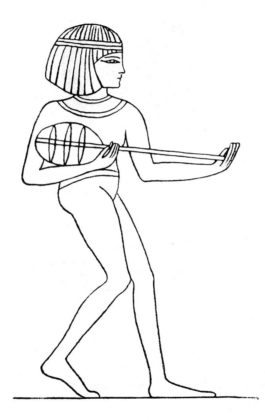

Fig. 48

Fig. 49

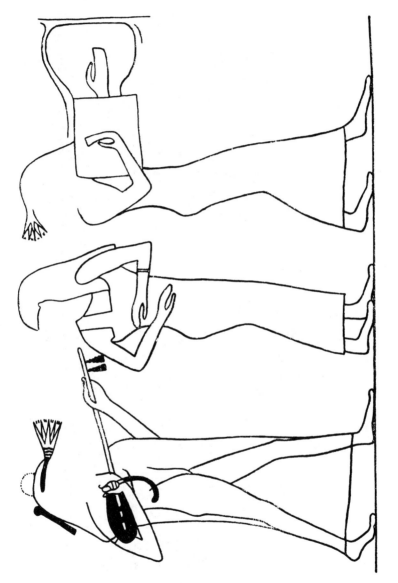

Fig. 50

134

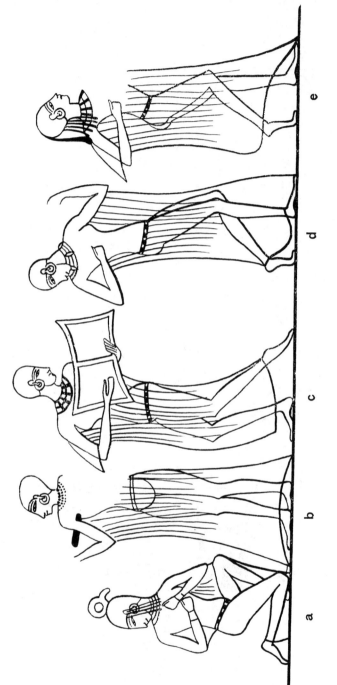

a   b   c   d   e

Fig. 51

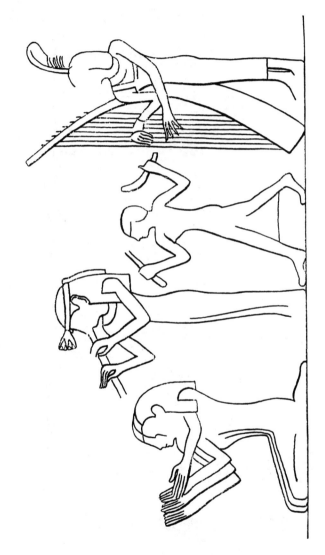

Fig. 52

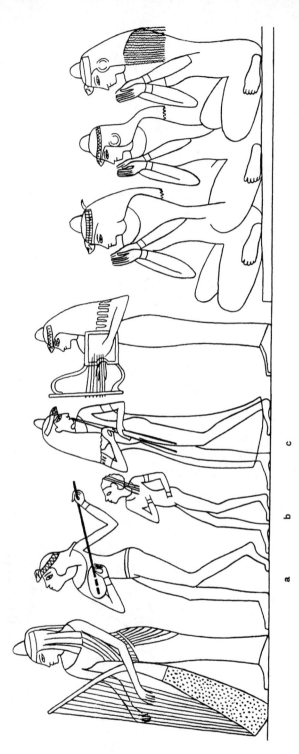

Fig. 53

a   b   c

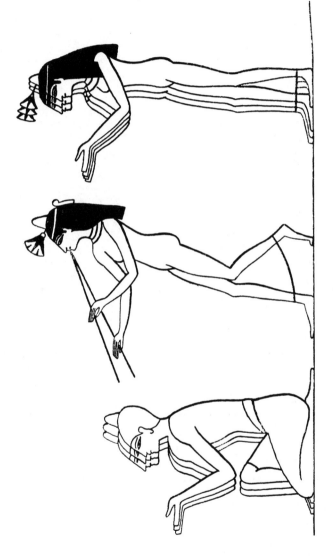

Fig. 54

Fig. 55

a   b   c

Fig. 56

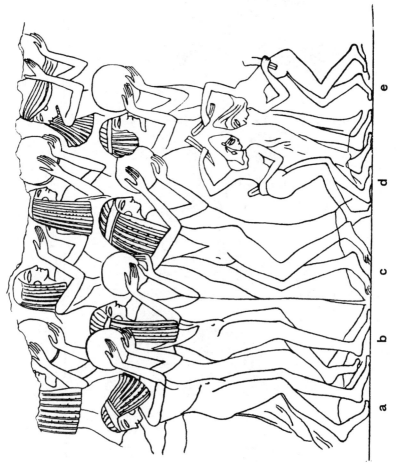

Fig. 57

140

Fig. 58

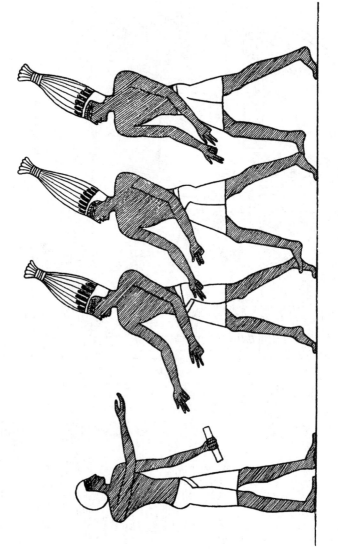

Fig. 59

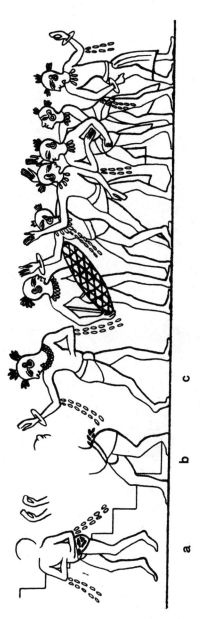

Fig. 60

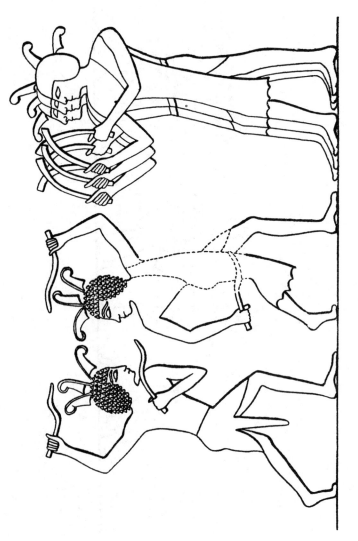

Fig. 61

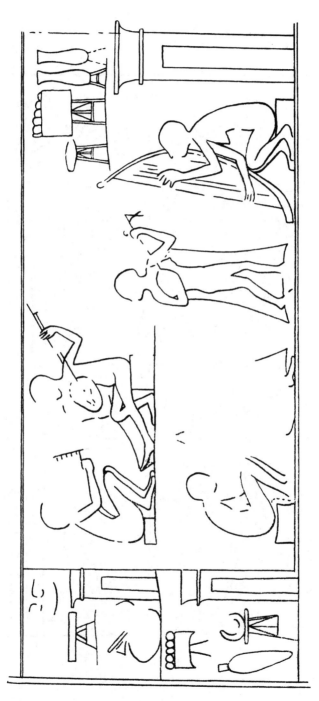

Fig. 62

Fig. 63

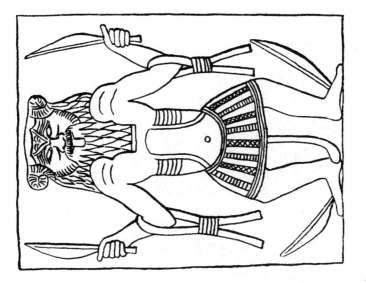

Fig. 64

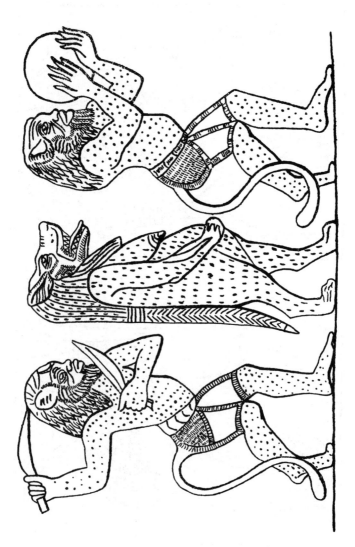

Fig. 65

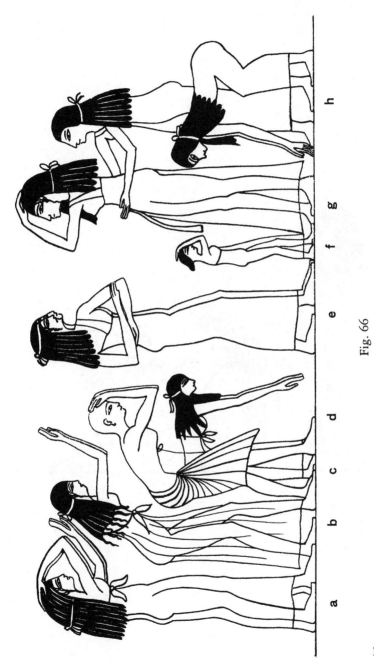

Fig. 66

Fig. 67

a   b

Fig. 68

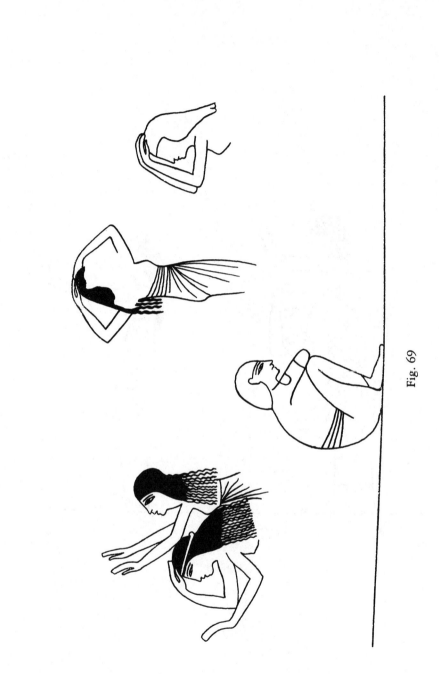

Fig. 69

Fig. 70

Fig. 71

Fig. 72

Fig. 73

Fig. 74

Figs. 75–76

Fig. 77

Fig. 78

A CATALOG OF SELECTED
DOVER BOOKS
IN ALL FIELDS OF INTEREST

A CATALOG OF SELECTED DOVER
BOOKS IN ALL FIELDS OF INTEREST

CONCERNING THE SPIRITUAL IN ART, Wassily Kandinsky. Pioneering work by father of abstract art. Thoughts on color theory, nature of art. Analysis of earlier masters. 12 illustrations. 80pp. of text. 5⅜ x 8½. 23411-8

ANIMALS: 1,419 Copyright-Free Illustrations of Mammals, Birds, Fish, Insects, etc., Jim Harter (ed.). Clear wood engravings present, in extremely lifelike poses, over 1,000 species of animals. One of the most extensive pictorial sourcebooks of its kind. Captions. Index. 284pp. 9 x 12. 23766-4

CELTIC ART: The Methods of Construction, George Bain. Simple geometric techniques for making Celtic interlacements, spirals, Kells-type initials, animals, humans, etc. Over 500 illustrations. 160pp. 9 x 12. (Available in U.S. only.) 22923-8

AN ATLAS OF ANATOMY FOR ARTISTS, Fritz Schider. Most thorough reference work on art anatomy in the world. Hundreds of illustrations, including selections from works by Vesalius, Leonardo, Goya, Ingres, Michelangelo, others. 593 illustrations. 192pp. 7⅛ x 10¼. 20241-0

CELTIC HAND STROKE-BY-STROKE (Irish Half Uncial from "The Book of Kells"): An Arthur Baker Calligraphy Manual, Arthur Baker. Complete guide to creating each letter of the alphabet in distinctive Celtic manner. Covers hand position, strokes, pens, inks, paper, more. Illustrated. 48pp. 8¼ x 11. 24336-2

EASY ORIGAMI, John Montroll. Charming collection of 32 projects (hat, cup, pelican, piano, swan, many more) specially designed for the novice origami hobbyist. Clearly illustrated easy-to-follow instructions insure that even beginning papercrafters will achieve successful results. 48pp. 8¼ x 11. 27298-2

THE COMPLETE BOOK OF BIRDHOUSE CONSTRUCTION FOR WOOD-WORKERS, Scott D. Campbell. Detailed instructions, illustrations, tables. Also data on bird habitat and instinct patterns. Bibliography. 3 tables. 63 illustrations in 15 figures. 48pp. 5¼ x 8½. 24407-5

BLOOMINGDALE'S ILLUSTRATED 1886 CATALOG: Fashions, Dry Goods and Housewares, Bloomingdale Brothers. Famed merchants' extremely rare catalog depicting about 1,700 products: clothing, housewares, firearms, dry goods, jewelry, more. Invaluable for dating, identifying vintage items. Also, copyright-free graphics for artists, designers. Co-published with Henry Ford Museum & Greenfield Village. 160pp. 8¼ x 11. 25780-0

HISTORIC COSTUME IN PICTURES, Braun & Schneider. Over 1,450 costumed figures in clearly detailed engravings–from dawn of civilization to end of 19th century. Captions. Many folk costumes. 256pp. 8⅜ x 11¾. 23150-X

THE CLARINET AND CLARINET PLAYING, David Pino. Lively, comprehensive work features suggestions about technique, musicianship, and musical interpretation, as well as guidelines for teaching, making your own reeds, and preparing for public performance. Includes an intriguing look at clarinet history. "A godsend," *The Clarinet,* Journal of the International Clarinet Society. Appendixes. 7 illus. 320pp. 5⅜ x 8½. 40270-3

HOLLYWOOD GLAMOR PORTRAITS, John Kobal (ed.). 145 photos from 1926-49. Harlow, Gable, Bogart, Bacall; 94 stars in all. Full background on photographers, technical aspects. 160pp. 8⅜ x 11¼. 23352-9

THE ANNOTATED CASEY AT THE BAT: A Collection of Ballads about the Mighty Casey/Third, Revised Edition, Martin Gardner (ed.). Amusing sequels and parodies of one of America's best-loved poems: Casey's Revenge, Why Casey Whiffed, Casey's Sister at the Bat, others. 256pp. 5⅜ x 8½. 28598-7

THE RAVEN AND OTHER FAVORITE POEMS, Edgar Allan Poe. Over 40 of the author's most memorable poems: "The Bells," "Ulalume," "Israfel," "To Helen," "The Conqueror Worm," "Eldorado," "Annabel Lee," many more. Alphabetic lists of titles and first lines. 64pp. $5\frac{3}{16}$ x 8¼. 26685-0

PERSONAL MEMOIRS OF U. S. GRANT, Ulysses Simpson Grant. Intelligent, deeply moving firsthand account of Civil War campaigns, considered by many the finest military memoirs ever written. Includes letters, historic photographs, maps and more. 528pp. 6⅛ x 9¼. 28587-1

ANCIENT EGYPTIAN MATERIALS AND INDUSTRIES, A. Lucas and J. Harris. Fascinating, comprehensive, thoroughly documented text describes this ancient civilization's vast resources and the processes that incorporated them in daily life, including the use of animal products, building materials, cosmetics, perfumes and incense, fibers, glazed ware, glass and its manufacture, materials used in the mummification process, and much more. 544pp. 6⅛ x 9¼. (Available in U.S. only.) 40446-3

RUSSIAN STORIES/RUSSKIE RASSKAZY: A Dual-Language Book, edited by Gleb Struve. Twelve tales by such masters as Chekhov, Tolstoy, Dostoevsky, Pushkin, others. Excellent word-for-word English translations on facing pages, plus teaching and study aids, Russian/English vocabulary, biographical/critical introductions, more. 416pp. 5⅜ x 8½. 26244-8

PHILADELPHIA THEN AND NOW: 60 Sites Photographed in the Past and Present, Kenneth Finkel and Susan Oyama. Rare photographs of City Hall, Logan Square, Independence Hall, Betsy Ross House, other landmarks juxtaposed with contemporary views. Captures changing face of historic city. Introduction. Captions. 128pp. 8¼ x 11. 25790-8

AIA ARCHITECTURAL GUIDE TO NASSAU AND SUFFOLK COUNTIES, LONG ISLAND, The American Institute of Architects, Long Island Chapter, and the Society for the Preservation of Long Island Antiquities. Comprehensive, well-researched and generously illustrated volume brings to life over three centuries of Long Island's great architectural heritage. More than 240 photographs with authoritative, extensively detailed captions. 176pp. 8¼ x 11. 26946-9

NORTH AMERICAN INDIAN LIFE: Customs and Traditions of 23 Tribes, Elsie Clews Parsons (ed.). 27 fictionalized essays by noted anthropologists examine religion, customs, government, additional facets of life among the Winnebago, Crow, Zuni, Eskimo, other tribes. 480pp. 6⅛ x 9¼. 27377-6

STICKLEY CRAFTSMAN FURNITURE CATALOGS, Gustav Stickley and L. & J. G. Stickley. Beautiful, functional furniture in two authentic catalogs from 1910. 594 illustrations, including 277 photos, show settles, rockers, armchairs, reclining chairs, bookcases, desks, tables. 183pp. 6½ x 9¼. 23838-5

AMERICAN LOCOMOTIVES IN HISTORIC PHOTOGRAPHS: 1858 to 1949, Ron Ziel (ed.). A rare collection of 126 meticulously detailed official photographs, called "builder portraits," of American locomotives that majestically chronicle the rise of steam locomotive power in America. Introduction. Detailed captions. xi+ 129pp. 9 x 12. 27393-8

AMERICA'S LIGHTHOUSES: An Illustrated History, Francis Ross Holland, Jr. Delightfully written, profusely illustrated fact-filled survey of over 200 American lighthouses since 1716. History, anecdotes, technological advances, more. 240pp. 8 x 10¾. 25576-X

TOWARDS A NEW ARCHITECTURE, Le Corbusier. Pioneering manifesto by founder of "International School." Technical and aesthetic theories, views of industry, economics, relation of form to function, "mass-production split" and much more. Profusely illustrated. 320pp. 6⅛ x 9¼. (Available in U.S. only.) 25023-7

HOW THE OTHER HALF LIVES, Jacob Riis. Famous journalistic record, exposing poverty and degradation of New York slums around 1900, by major social reformer. 100 striking and influential photographs. 233pp. 10 x 7⅞. 22012-5

FRUIT KEY AND TWIG KEY TO TREES AND SHRUBS, William M. Harlow. One of the handiest and most widely used identification aids. Fruit key covers 120 deciduous and evergreen species; twig key 160 deciduous species. Easily used. Over 300 photographs. 126pp. 5⅜ x 8½. 20511-8

COMMON BIRD SONGS, Dr. Donald J. Borror. Songs of 60 most common U.S. birds: robins, sparrows, cardinals, bluejays, finches, more—arranged in order of increasing complexity. Up to 9 variations of songs of each species.
Cassette and manual 99911-4

ORCHIDS AS HOUSE PLANTS, Rebecca Tyson Northen. Grow cattleyas and many other kinds of orchids—in a window, in a case, or under artificial light. 63 illustrations. 148pp. 5⅜ x 8½. 23261-1

MONSTER MAZES, Dave Phillips. Masterful mazes at four levels of difficulty. Avoid deadly perils and evil creatures to find magical treasures. Solutions for all 32 exciting illustrated puzzles. 48pp. 8¼ x 11. 26005-4

MOZART'S DON GIOVANNI (DOVER OPERA LIBRETTO SERIES), Wolfgang Amadeus Mozart. Introduced and translated by Ellen H. Bleiler. Standard Italian libretto, with complete English translation. Convenient and thoroughly portable—an ideal companion for reading along with a recording or the performance itself. Introduction. List of characters. Plot summary. 121pp. 5¼ x 8½. 24944-1

TECHNICAL MANUAL AND DICTIONARY OF CLASSICAL BALLET, Gail Grant. Defines, explains, comments on steps, movements, poses and concepts. 15-page pictorial section. Basic book for student, viewer. 127pp. 5⅜ x 8½. 21843-0

FRANK LLOYD WRIGHT'S DANA HOUSE, Donald Hoffmann. Pictorial essay of residential masterpiece with over 160 interior and exterior photos, plans, elevations, sketches and studies. 128pp. 9¼ x 10¾. 29120-0

THE MALE AND FEMALE FIGURE IN MOTION: 60 Classic Photographic Sequences, Eadweard Muybridge. 60 true-action photographs of men and women walking, running, climbing, bending, turning, etc., reproduced from rare 19th-century masterpiece. vi + 121pp. 9 x 12. 24745-7

1001 QUESTIONS ANSWERED ABOUT THE SEASHORE, N. J. Berrill and Jacquelyn Berrill. Queries answered about dolphins, sea snails, sponges, starfish, fishes, shore birds, many others. Covers appearance, breeding, growth, feeding, much more. 305pp. 5¼ x 8¼. 23366-9

ATTRACTING BIRDS TO YOUR YARD, William J. Weber. Easy-to-follow guide offers advice on how to attract the greatest diversity of birds: birdhouses, feeders, water and waterers, much more. 96pp. 5³⁄₁₆ x 8¼. 28927-3

MEDICINAL AND OTHER USES OF NORTH AMERICAN PLANTS: A Historical Survey with Special Reference to the Eastern Indian Tribes, Charlotte Erichsen-Brown. Chronological historical citations document 500 years of usage of plants, trees, shrubs native to eastern Canada, northeastern U.S. Also complete identifying information. 343 illustrations. 544pp. 6½ x 9¼. 25951-X

STORYBOOK MAZES, Dave Phillips. 23 stories and mazes on two-page spreads: Wizard of Oz, Treasure Island, Robin Hood, etc. Solutions. 64pp. 8¼ x 11. 23628-5

AMERICAN NEGRO SONGS: 230 Folk Songs and Spirituals, Religious and Secular, John W. Work. This authoritative study traces the African influences of songs sung and played by black Americans at work, in church, and as entertainment. The author discusses the lyric significance of such songs as "Swing Low, Sweet Chariot," "John Henry," and others and offers the words and music for 230 songs. Bibliography. Index of Song Titles. 272pp. 6½ x 9¼. 40271-1

MOVIE-STAR PORTRAITS OF THE FORTIES, John Kobal (ed.). 163 glamor, studio photos of 106 stars of the 1940s: Rita Hayworth, Ava Gardner, Marlon Brando, Clark Gable, many more. 176pp. 8⅜ x 11¼. 23546-7

BENCHLEY LOST AND FOUND, Robert Benchley. Finest humor from early 30s, about pet peeves, child psychologists, post office and others. Mostly unavailable elsewhere. 73 illustrations by Peter Arno and others. 183pp. 5⅜ x 8½. 22410-4

YEKL and THE IMPORTED BRIDEGROOM AND OTHER STORIES OF YIDDISH NEW YORK, Abraham Cahan. Film Hester Street based on *Yekl* (1896). Novel, other stories among first about Jewish immigrants on N.Y.'s East Side. 240pp. 5⅜ x 8½. 22427-9

SELECTED POEMS, Walt Whitman. Generous sampling from *Leaves of Grass*. Twenty-four poems include "I Hear America Singing," "Song of the Open Road," "I Sing the Body Electric," "When Lilacs Last in the Dooryard Bloom'd," "O Captain! My Captain!"–all reprinted from an authoritative edition. Lists of titles and first lines. 128pp. 5³⁄₁₆ x 8¼. 26878-0

THE BEST TALES OF HOFFMANN, E. T. A. Hoffmann. 10 of Hoffmann's most important stories: "Nutcracker and the King of Mice," "The Golden Flowerpot," etc. 458pp. 5⅜ x 8½. 21793-0

FROM FETISH TO GOD IN ANCIENT EGYPT, E. A. Wallis Budge. Rich detailed survey of Egyptian conception of "God" and gods, magic, cult of animals, Osiris, more. Also, superb English translations of hymns and legends. 240 illustrations. 545pp. 5⅜ x 8½. 25803-3

FRENCH STORIES/CONTES FRANÇAIS: A Dual-Language Book, Wallace Fowlie. Ten stories by French masters, Voltaire to Camus: "Micromegas" by Voltaire; "The Atheist's Mass" by Balzac; "Minuet" by de Maupassant; "The Guest" by Camus, six more. Excellent English translations on facing pages. Also French-English vocabulary list, exercises, more. 352pp. 5⅜ x 8½. 26443-2

CHICAGO AT THE TURN OF THE CENTURY IN PHOTOGRAPHS: 122 Historic Views from the Collections of the Chicago Historical Society, Larry A. Viskochil. Rare large-format prints offer detailed views of City Hall, State Street, the Loop, Hull House, Union Station, many other landmarks, circa 1904-1913. Introduction. Captions. Maps. 144pp. 9⅜ x 12¼. 24656-6

OLD BROOKLYN IN EARLY PHOTOGRAPHS, 1865-1929, William Lee Younger. Luna Park, Gravesend race track, construction of Grand Army Plaza, moving of Hotel Brighton, etc. 157 previously unpublished photographs. 165pp. 8⅞ x 11¾. 23587-4

THE MYTHS OF THE NORTH AMERICAN INDIANS, Lewis Spence. Rich anthology of the myths and legends of the Algonquins, Iroquois, Pawnees and Sioux, prefaced by an extensive historical and ethnological commentary. 36 illustrations. 480pp. 5⅜ x 8½. 25967-6

AN ENCYCLOPEDIA OF BATTLES: Accounts of Over 1,560 Battles from 1479 B.C. to the Present, David Eggenberger. Essential details of every major battle in recorded history from the first battle of Megiddo in 1479 B.C. to Grenada in 1984. List of Battle Maps. New Appendix covering the years 1967-1984. Index. 99 illustrations. 544pp. 6½ x 9¼. 24913-1

SAILING ALONE AROUND THE WORLD, Captain Joshua Slocum. First man to sail around the world, alone, in small boat. One of great feats of seamanship told in delightful manner. 67 illustrations. 294pp. 5⅜ x 8½. 20326-3

ANARCHISM AND OTHER ESSAYS, Emma Goldman. Powerful, penetrating, prophetic essays on direct action, role of minorities, prison reform, puritan hypocrisy, violence, etc. 271pp. 5⅜ x 8½. 22484-8

MYTHS OF THE HINDUS AND BUDDHISTS, Ananda K. Coomaraswamy and Sister Nivedita. Great stories of the epics; deeds of Krishna, Shiva, taken from puranas, Vedas, folk tales; etc. 32 illustrations. 400pp. 5⅜ x 8½. 21759-0

THE TRAUMA OF BIRTH, Otto Rank. Rank's controversial thesis that anxiety neurosis is caused by profound psychological trauma which occurs at birth. 256pp. 5⅜ x 8½. 27974-X

A THEOLOGICO-POLITICAL TREATISE, Benedict Spinoza. Also contains unfinished Political Treatise. Great classic on religious liberty, theory of government on common consent. R. Elwes translation. Total of 421pp. 5⅜ x 8½. 20249-6

MY BONDAGE AND MY FREEDOM, Frederick Douglass. Born a slave, Douglass became outspoken force in antislavery movement. The best of Douglass' autobiographies. Graphic description of slave life. 464pp. 5⅜ x 8½.   22457-0

FOLLOWING THE EQUATOR: A Journey Around the World, Mark Twain. Fascinating humorous account of 1897 voyage to Hawaii, Australia, India, New Zealand, etc. Ironic, bemused reports on peoples, customs, climate, flora and fauna, politics, much more. 197 illustrations. 720pp. 5⅜ x 8½.   26113-1

THE PEOPLE CALLED SHAKERS, Edward D. Andrews. Definitive study of Shakers: origins, beliefs, practices, dances, social organization, furniture and crafts, etc. 33 illustrations. 351pp. 5⅜ x 8½.   21081-2

THE MYTHS OF GREECE AND ROME, H. A. Guerber. A classic of mythology, generously illustrated, long prized for its simple, graphic, accurate retelling of the principal myths of Greece and Rome, and for its commentary on their origins and significance. With 64 illustrations by Michelangelo, Raphael, Titian, Rubens, Canova, Bernini and others. 480pp. 5⅜ x 8½.   27584-1

PSYCHOLOGY OF MUSIC, Carl E. Seashore. Classic work discusses music as a medium from psychological viewpoint. Clear treatment of physical acoustics, auditory apparatus, sound perception, development of musical skills, nature of musical feeling, host of other topics. 88 figures. 408pp. 5⅜ x 8½.   21851-1

THE PHILOSOPHY OF HISTORY, Georg W. Hegel. Great classic of Western thought develops concept that history is not chance but rational process, the evolution of freedom. 457pp. 5⅜ x 8½.   20112-0

THE BOOK OF TEA, Kakuzo Okakura. Minor classic of the Orient: entertaining, charming explanation, interpretation of traditional Japanese culture in terms of tea ceremony. 94pp. 5⅜ x 8½.   20070-1

LIFE IN ANCIENT EGYPT, Adolf Erman. Fullest, most thorough, detailed older account with much not in more recent books, domestic life, religion, magic, medicine, commerce, much more. Many illustrations reproduce tomb paintings, carvings, hieroglyphs, etc. 597pp. 5⅜ x 8½.   22632-8

SUNDIALS, Their Theory and Construction, Albert Waugh. Far and away the best, most thorough coverage of ideas, mathematics concerned, types, construction, adjusting anywhere. Simple, nontechnical treatment allows even children to build several of these dials. Over 100 illustrations. 230pp. 5⅜ x 8½.   22947-5

THEORETICAL HYDRODYNAMICS, L. M. Milne-Thomson. Classic exposition of the mathematical theory of fluid motion, applicable to both hydrodynamics and aerodynamics. Over 600 exercises. 768pp. 6⅛ x 9¼.   68970-0

SONGS OF EXPERIENCE: Facsimile Reproduction with 26 Plates in Full Color, William Blake. 26 full-color plates from a rare 1826 edition. Includes "The Tyger," "London," "Holy Thursday," and other poems. Printed text of poems. 48pp. 5¼ x 7.   24636-1

OLD-TIME VIGNETTES IN FULL COLOR, Carol Belanger Grafton (ed.). Over 390 charming, often sentimental illustrations, selected from archives of Victorian graphics—pretty women posing, children playing, food, flowers, kittens and puppies, smiling cherubs, birds and butterflies, much more. All copyright-free. 48pp. 9¼ x 12¼.   27269-9

PERSPECTIVE FOR ARTISTS, Rex Vicat Cole. Depth, perspective of sky and sea, shadows, much more, not usually covered. 391 diagrams, 81 reproductions of drawings and paintings. 279pp. 5⅜ x 8½. 22487-2

DRAWING THE LIVING FIGURE, Joseph Sheppard. Innovative approach to artistic anatomy focuses on specifics of surface anatomy, rather than muscles and bones. Over 170 drawings of live models in front, back and side views, and in widely varying poses. Accompanying diagrams. 177 illustrations. Introduction. Index. 144pp. 8⅜ x11¼. 26723-7

GOTHIC AND OLD ENGLISH ALPHABETS: 100 Complete Fonts, Dan X. Solo. Add power, elegance to posters, signs, other graphics with 100 stunning copyright-free alphabets: Blackstone, Dolbey, Germania, 97 more—including many lower-case, numerals, punctuation marks. 104pp. 8⅛ x 11. 24695-7

HOW TO DO BEADWORK, Mary White. Fundamental book on craft from simple projects to five-bead chains and woven works. 106 illustrations. 142pp. 5⅜ x 8.
20697-1

THE BOOK OF WOOD CARVING, Charles Marshall Sayers. Finest book for beginners discusses fundamentals and offers 34 designs. "Absolutely first rate . . . well thought out and well executed."—E. J. Tangerman. 118pp. 7¾ x 10⅝. 23654-4

ILLUSTRATED CATALOG OF CIVIL WAR MILITARY GOODS: Union Army Weapons, Insignia, Uniform Accessories, and Other Equipment, Schuyler, Hartley, and Graham. Rare, profusely illustrated 1846 catalog includes Union Army uniform and dress regulations, arms and ammunition, coats, insignia, flags, swords, rifles, etc. 226 illustrations. 160pp. 9 x 12. 24939-5

WOMEN'S FASHIONS OF THE EARLY 1900s: An Unabridged Republication of "New York Fashions, 1909," National Cloak & Suit Co. Rare catalog of mail-order fashions documents women's and children's clothing styles shortly after the turn of the century. Captions offer full descriptions, prices. Invaluable resource for fashion, costume historians. Approximately 725 illustrations. 128pp. 8⅜ x 11¼. 27276-1

THE 1912 AND 1915 GUSTAV STICKLEY FURNITURE CATALOGS, Gustav Stickley. With over 200 detailed illustrations and descriptions, these two catalogs are essential reading and reference materials and identification guides for Stickley furniture. Captions cite materials, dimensions and prices. 112pp. 6½ x 9¼. 26676-1

EARLY AMERICAN LOCOMOTIVES, John H. White, Jr. Finest locomotive engravings from early 19th century: historical (1804–74), main-line (after 1870), special, foreign, etc. 147 plates. 142pp. 11⅜ x 8¼. 22772-3

THE TALL SHIPS OF TODAY IN PHOTOGRAPHS, Frank O. Braynard. Lavishly illustrated tribute to nearly 100 majestic contemporary sailing vessels: Amerigo Vespucci, Clearwater, Constitution, Eagle, Mayflower, Sea Cloud, Victory, many more. Authoritative captions provide statistics, background on each ship. 190 black-and-white photographs and illustrations. Introduction. 128pp. 8⅞ x 11¾.
27163-3

CATALOG OF DOVER BOOKS

THE STORY OF THE TITANIC AS TOLD BY ITS SURVIVORS, Jack Winocour (ed.). What it was really like. Panic, despair, shocking inefficiency, and a little hero-ism. More thrilling than any fictional account. 26 illustrations. 320pp. 5⅜ x 8½.
20610-6

FAIRY AND FOLK TALES OF THE IRISH PEASANTRY, William Butler Yeats (ed.). Treasury of 64 tales from the twilight world of Celtic myth and legend: "The Soul Cages," "The Kildare Pooka," "King O'Toole and his Goose," many more. Introduction and Notes by W. B. Yeats. 352pp. 5⅜ x 8½.
26941-8

BUDDHIST MAHAYANA TEXTS, E. B. Cowell and others (eds.). Superb, accu-rate translations of basic documents in Mahayana Buddhism, highly important in his-tory of religions. The Buddha-karita of Asvaghosha, Larger Sukhavativyuha, more. 448pp. 5⅜ x 8½.
25552-2

ONE TWO THREE . . . INFINITY: Facts and Speculations of Science, George Gamow. Great physicist's fascinating, readable overview of contemporary science: number theory, relativity, fourth dimension, entropy, genes, atomic structure, much more. 128 illustrations. Index. 352pp. 5⅜ x 8½.
25664-2

EXPERIMENTATION AND MEASUREMENT, W. J. Youden. Introductory man-ual explains laws of measurement in simple terms and offers tips for achieving accu-racy and minimizing errors. Mathematics of measurement, use of instruments, exper-imenting with machines. 1994 edition. Foreword. Preface. Introduction. Epilogue. Selected Readings. Glossary. Index. Tables and figures. 128pp. 5⅜ x 8½.   40451-X

DALÍ ON MODERN ART: The Cuckolds of Antiquated Modern Art, Salvador Dalí. Influential painter skewers modern art and its practitioners. Outrageous evaluations of Picasso, Cézanne, Turner, more. 15 renderings of paintings discussed. 44 calligraphic decorations by Dalí. 96pp. 5⅜ x 8½. (Available in U.S. only.)   29220-7

ANTIQUE PLAYING CARDS: A Pictorial History, Henry René D'Allemagne. Over 900 elaborate, decorative images from rare playing cards (14th–20th centuries): Bacchus, death, dancing dogs, hunting scenes, royal coats of arms, players cheating, much more. 96pp. 9¼ x 12¼.
29265-7

MAKING FURNITURE MASTERPIECES: 30 Projects with Measured Drawings, Franklin H. Gottshall. Step-by-step instructions, illustrations for constructing hand-some, useful pieces, among them a Sheraton desk, Chippendale chair, Spanish desk, Queen Anne table and a William and Mary dressing mirror. 224pp. 8⅛ x 11¼.
29338-6

THE FOSSIL BOOK: A Record of Prehistoric Life, Patricia V. Rich et al. Profusely illustrated definitive guide covers everything from single-celled organisms and dinosaurs to birds and mammals and the interplay between climate and man. Over 1,500 illustrations. 760pp. 7½ x 10⅛.
29371-8

Paperbound unless otherwise indicated. Available at your book dealer, online at **www.doverpublications.com**, or by writing to Dept. GI, Dover Publications, Inc., 31 East 2nd Street, Mineola, NY 11501. For current price information or for free catalogues (please indicate field of interest), write to Dover Publications or log on to **www.doverpublications.com** and see every Dover book in print. Dover publishes more than 500 books each year on science, elementary and advanced mathematics, biology, music, art, literary history, social sciences, and other areas.